FUNDAMENTAL

COLLEGE

COMPOSITION

FUNDAMENTAL COLLEGE COMPOSITION

WILLIAM P. DE FEO

Assistant Professor
The Ancell School of Business
Division of Justice and Law Administration
Western Connecticut State University

BrownWalker Press
Irvine • Boca Raton

Fundamental College Composition

BrownWalker Press / Universal Publishers, Inc.
Irvine • Boca Raton
USA • 2017
www.universal-publishers.com

978-1-62734-687-0 (pbk.)
978-1-62734-688-7 (ebk.)

Typeset by Medlar Publishing Solutions Pvt Ltd, India

Publisher's Cataloging-in-Publication Data

Names: DeFeo, William P.
Title: Fundamental college composition / William P. DeFeo.
Description: Edition. | Irvine, CA : BrownWalker, 2017.
Identifiers: LCCN 2017950762 | ISBN 978-1-62734-687-0 (pbk.) | ISBN 978-1-62734-688-7 (ebook)
Subjects: LCSH: English language--Composition and exercises. | English language--Grammar--Handbooks, manuals, etc. | English language--Rhetoric--Handbooks, manuals, etc. | Education, Higher. | Academic achievement. | BISAC: LANGUAGE ARTS & DISCIPLINES / Composition & Creative Writing. | LANGUAGE ARTS & DISCIPLINES / Grammar & Punctuation. | EDUCATION / Higher.
Classification: LCC PE1408 .D394 2017 (print) | LCC PE1408 (ebook) | DDC 808/.042--dc23.

This book is dedicated to my family

in the order of importance

set forth under

the Common Law Rules of Consanguinity

for Intestate Descent and Distribution of Estates.

TABLE OF CONTENTS

FOREWORD

This is a book about writing. It presumes to make plain to the college level student the mysteries of good writing. It hopes to do so briefly and efficiently, but brevity and efficiency are not chums; things done quickly are not usually done well. Nevertheless, my plan is that this volume will be a notable exception to that rule. In a relatively short space, it will reveal the fundamentals of sound college composition. Writing a textbook on any subject is a challenging task because the final product needs to be instructional. Conventional books can inform or entertain; textbooks must teach. Even with the aid of a very competent instructor, good textbooks must clear a high pedagogical bar.

Writing a college level textbook about writing shoulders an additional burden. A college writing textbook must teach, but it must teach material that students often believe they already know well enough. Most college students have been writing successfully for more than a decade, and many others for much longer. A textbook that presumes to teach college level writing needs to overcome the significant obstacle of compositional complacency – the belief that adequate writing skills are....adequate, and that improvement in the use of language arts is unnecessary. This "adequacy mindset" is a prodigious villain with which the writing writer must do battle.

In addition, many troubling questions present themselves. How will the writing textbook present timelessly old material in new and interesting ways? How will the book meet its primary objective to demonstrably improve student writing? In a culture crowded with sound bites, insta-grams, texting, and hand-held devices that intuit what a writer thinks even before the keys are touched, how can a conventional book ever succeed? How does any book or any teacher seriously propose to convince 21st century students accustomed to fast-lane living that they need to slow down? And when the message is delivered – the message that good writing demands slow, deliberate, often painful effort – how can a teacher reasonably expect a student to respond affirmatively? What possible persuasions can the author of a writing textbook use to win the hearts and minds of modern, speed-conscious learners when those learners discover that writing one, well-constructed paragraph may often demand the better part of an hour of writing and revision?

These have always been difficult questions. They become even more difficult in a digital, and perhaps soon to be a quantum, computing age where delivering a message quickly has become more important than constructing a message that is clear, precise and unambiguous.

Whatever the answers to these questions may be – and my answers to them will be offered in different parts of the text – certain truths remain inviolate; good writing has value, people capable of producing good writing are increasingly scarce, and scarcity makes good writers very valuable commodities. Students who apply themselves to learning the skills necessary to become good writers will flourish in every professional and many non-professional fields. This is a strong argument in favor of learning to write well. Of course, as Shakespeare explained, "If to do were as easy as to know what were good to do, chapels had been churches..." (The Merchant of Venice, I, ii, 12-13). The student may know that learning to write well is a good thing to do, but the mere knowing does not get the doing done.

At the beginning of any academic pursuit, honesty and truth are best. Therefore let us honestly acknowledge a hard truth; reading a college textbook is almost always an exercise in tedium. For one reason it is an imposed, not a voluntary, labor. For another, reading a textbook usually draws the reader into still further imposed, involuntary labors. Understanding terse definitions, digesting entangled concepts, and completing programmed writing exercises are just some of the many irritating elements of a college writing text. There is no point in trying to deceive ourselves. We know in our heart of hearts that squaring our shoulders to academic difficulty and working our way through it are the only true paths to learning.

This book will teach writing to those who confront and overcome that difficulty by reading and studying the text. Without careful reading and determined study, this book will fail and the promise of learning it holds for the student will be jealously and appropriately withheld. There is no substitute for hard work. Successful athletes and accomplished musicians and artists know this well; they are not born, they are made. The endless repetitive drills that painfully produce the slowly emerging skills must be undertaken with determination and as much good cheer as possible. An abundance of natural talent is a very fine thing, but it is no substitute for focused, deliberate, unrelenting labor. After a particularly brilliant performance, a famed international American-born pianist was approached by a fan who adoringly said, "I would give everything in my life to play the piano the way you do." Without the slightest hesitation, the artist replied, "I did."

Students may rest assured I will invest the time and energy to make the text as effective as my skills allow. However, I must seek assurance from each student reader that they will invest their time and energy and allow the book to give them all it has to offer.

At the end of the book I will provide an Afterword that will evaluate how closely I believe the book has come to meeting its intention to teach writing. However, a good part of our human nature is our self-interest and conceit, and so I strongly suspect the Afterword will reveal that my book has been wonderfully successful. Nevertheless, the only true evaluation of a book that teaches is a reader that learns, and so the reader's success and the author's success are interdependent. It appears we both have our work to do. Education may well be a labor of love, but it is labor nonetheless, and very shortly you and I will be left to do our work.

I will begin my labor by thanking my wife for helping me to maintain the presence of mind I will need to complete this text. Her cool patience and iron strength are frightening things, yet they have supported and sustained me in all I have done. I hope she will continue her vigilance through completion of this volume. If she does not, I will make particular note of it in the Afterword.

Danbury, Connecticut
WPD 2017

A NOTE ON CHAPTER NUTSHELLS
AND CHAPTER EXERCISES

At the end of each chapter the student will see two concluding elements: a "chapter nutshell" and a "chapter exercise." They are provided to assist understanding and application of each chapter's materials.

The nutshell will attempt to reduce each chapter's important points to a few concise sentences. Nutshells are not provided as alternatives to reading and understanding the chapters. Rather, they are in the nature of study aides that can help students quickly refresh their recollection of the major chapter elements. If the nutshells succeed in jogging student memory and bringing back into focus chapter details, they will fulfill their primary objective.

A chapter exercise will follow each of the nutshells. Each exercise is brief and clearly explained. The exercise will direct the student to first access and then carefully read a short sample of world-class writing from an author who has stood the test of time. Once the sample has been read and understood, the student will be prompted to compose a brief essay not to exceed one hundred words that follows the instruction of the particular prompt.

These exercises are specifically designed to stretch the student's reading comprehension and writing skills to the uttermost. They will also provide the course instructor with a valid assessment tool. The reading samples often contain dense, complex ideas expressed in varying writing styles that will challenge most college level readers. Some students may struggle to understand the sample writings, but struggle that promises illumination is worth the burden. Learning to improve writing skills is a vigorous undertaking. The successful student will not shrink from the prospect of intellectual struggle, but approach it with dogged determination.

Permit me to run contrary to much modern pedagogy and modestly make the following suggestion. As you read the selections assigned in the chapter exercises you may very possibly come across a few lines or sentences that resonate in your heart or mind. Memorize them! With a very little effort, you will have a treasure in your pocket for a lifetime. Today memorization is not held in high educational esteem. It is considered too structured and too disciplined. On the contrary, structure and discipline have never been enemies of learning.

CHAPTER ONE

THE LANGUAGE STUDY ARGUMENT

All college students possess a familiarity with the elements of language arts. This familiarity ranges from a very mild, passing acquaintance at one end, to a deep and abiding love of language at the other. In between these extremes lie a myriad of degrees. The purpose of this book is to draw all students closer to that love of the art of language – a love that should be stronger than their love of music, of art, of literature, of science, of mathematics, or even of sweet philosophy. That may seem far too ambitious a purpose for a book of grammar, but it is not. Language art is the seed and soil of all thought and all learning. It is the parent art of all consequent arts and deserves nothing less than the devoted, unconditional love we reserve for a beloved parent, for without language we remain silent, untutored children. We recall nothing, calculate nothing, and communicate nothing. Without language there is neither song nor science. Without language we become prisoners of our short-term memories, condemned to an isolation of knowing only what our senses tell us of the world at present. Even romantic love, with all its force and power, pales in the absence of language. Without language, romantic love becomes little more than coarse colorless biology.

Despite its name, the study of "language arts" contains many unartistic sub-structures. These include grammar, syntax, rhetoric, vocabulary, logic, and the various mechanical conventions of Standard Written English such as punctuation, spelling, sentence structure, agreement, paragraphing and style. These language elements are seldom the chosen valentines of students. Nevertheless, they are unarguably the building blocks of sound composition. When we possess them, we have what we need to be good writers. They represent a body of knowledge without which improvement in writing is simply not possible. Natural ability and having "a good ear" for language may go far in helping to develop good writing skills, but taking the full tour and marveling at the buttresses and arches that support the grand architecture of good writing is an academic pursuit well worth the time.

And acquiring this body of knowledge will yield results far beyond improved writing. Good writers are almost always good speakers. Few of us will earn our bread as professional writers, but everyone can benefit from speaking well. The benefits of improved expression are practical things. Earning potential invariably increases for those who can speak well, who can explain what is complex, who can take dense detailed information and communicate it to others clearly and simply.

Written and spoken words become rich and expressive when language arts become a regular part of our educational diet. Without an appreciation for the structures that underlie language – without some level of understanding their mysteries – our writing and speech are shallow, diluted, and flavorless. Appreciate them and understand them, and you may take your reserved seat at the great feast of language.

Few authors have written about what writing is as well as Thomas Hobbes. As a philosopher, he ignores the frivolous and insubstantial and goes directly to the "pith and marrow." Reproduced below (with its original spellings and punctuation) is an excerpt from the introduction to the fourth chapter of Hobbes' book entitled *The Leviathan*.

The invention of *Printing*, though ingenious, compared with the invention of *Letters*, is no great matter. But who was the first that found the use of Letters, is not known. He that first brought them into *Greece*, men say was *Cadmus*, the sonne of *Agenor*, King of Phaenicia. A profitable invention for the continuing the memory of time past, and the conjunction of mankind, dispersed into so many, and distant regions of the Earth; and with all difficult, as proceeding from a watchful observation of the divers motions of the Tongue, Palat, Lips, and other organs of Speech; whereby to make as many differences of characters, to remember them. But the most noble and profitable invention of all other, was that of SPEECH, consisting of *Names* or *Appellations*, and their Connection. whereby men register their Thoughts; recall them when they are past; and also declare them one to another for

> mutuall utility and conversation; without which, there had been amongst men, neither Common-wealth, nor Society, nor Contract, nor Peace, no more than amongst Lyons, Bears and Wolves. (Hobbes, *Leviathan*)

This is a shining, albeit complex, example of our very own English language written circa 1630. You may imagine that the spell-check and grammar-check functions of my computer were given a strenuous workout when I entered this quotation. Yes, some of the words and spellings may be unfamiliar, but the idea is a consummate illumination: Speech, and its child, "Letters" (writing) utterly and particularly distinguish our species. Language arts have made possible all that is noble in us.

Perhaps you have never seriously applied yourself to the study of language arts. The work you might have done in grade school or high school may have been avoided. The subject may have never been systematically presented, or if it was, it may not have been aggressively or appropriately taught. In any event, this volume calls you to embrace the subject now.

As an older, more mature learner you will absorb and retain the challenging content more easily. The rewards of your study will be tangible, visible things, such as improved writing, precise speech, and persuasive communication. Your investment of time and study will pay dividends that younger students do not recognize and cannot appreciate – better grades, better jobs, and expanding career opportunities. These are sweeping claims, but language study has the temerity to make them, and a long, bold history that proves they can be attained by those who are resolved.

This volume is not a complete study of language art. It is admittedly sprinkled with the shortcomings of its author. Nevertheless, it will present the materials necessary for the conscientious student to secure a solid foundation for improving both academic and work-place writing. It will not presume too much student knowledge, but will presume some. Lengthy, repetitive drills and exercises have been replaced by specialized writing prompts that offer students opportunities to frame their developing skills. These prompts will showcase short, excerpted portions of selected exemplary writing samples from a broad range of academic sources. Students will be asked to use their skill to read, analyze, and finally interpret in their own words their understanding of the excerpt. In the author's humble opinion, focused, idea-driven writing exercises trump repetitive sentence-correcting writing drills every time.

One final point is worth special notice. Students may struggle with some of the vocabulary in this volume. The author does not apologize for selecting challenging words. They are the words that well-read, college level students should either be familiar with or be exposed to without further delay. In many cases, the context of the sentence will help readers divine the meanings of these words. In any case, an author's glossary is provided at the end of the book as a quick, relatively painless reference guide.

Mastery of rules and sharpened memory remain cornerstones of language proficiency. This book is no "genie's lamp." A strenuous rub of the cover will summon forth nothing. It is a book of complex, interwoven rules. Unraveling and digesting them demands a patient and careful application of the mind. Anything less will not yield a satisfactory result. And now that the book's groundwork has been laid and the argument for conscientious study is made, we can launch into the studies themselves.

***

Chapter One Nutshell

Human language is composed of multiple layers of speech, thought, and tactile skill. Learning to write well demands a significant investment of time. There are many "short-cuts" available to writing students. Unfortunately none of them work. Read much and write often.

Chapter One Exercise

Carefully re-read the quotation from Thomas Hobbes' philosophical treatise, *The Leviathan* provided in this chapter. Hobbes shares his thoughts with us about three elements of language, namely, printing, speech, and writing. In a paragraph of not more than 100 words, explain precisely what Hobbes is saying about those three elements. If his meaning is not clear to you, re-read the excerpt slowly and aloud several times. Do not use any direct quotation or paraphrase from any source.

CHAPTER TWO

PARTS OF SPEECH

Introduction

The study of human language is filled with irony. In a relatively short time after we are born, we learn how to use the sounds of words to our advantage and also learn how to listen and decipher the intentions behind the sounds of words used by others. All this learning happens of its own accord. We do not study language to become accomplished in those early years. A child's communication skills are unlearned and untutored. A bit later, school begins. We memorize our alphabet, along with the sounds of our native vowels and consonants, and begin a journey into the science of language. It is not too long after this – perhaps on the eve of an impending English test – that we are struck by the irony. A voice in us says stubbornly, "I know how to talk and I understand when others talk to me, so what is all this fuss about spelling, writing and these dreadful parts of speech?"

As the years pass we grudgingly realize that talking and listening are not enough. It is a simple matter of memory. There are just too many things we think, say, and hear to keep track of. If we don't record them somehow they'll be lost and we will have to think them or say them or hear them all over again. We know each of the ten items we need to buy at the store, but by the time our mind gets further toward the end of the list, we may not recall the items at the beginning. Using a stylus to make marks or symbols that represent the sounds of the items we want to buy is a great help. It keeps us from having to stop in the store aisle and bring to mind every item we want from memory. Somewhere far back in our ancestral past, our forbearers realized that making marks that bring to mind the sounds we learned as children, made remembering easier. Writing was born, and language art began. Parts of speech represent the first of many doors in the sprawling mansion of language art. They begin the atomistic deconstruction of this mammoth creature that Hobbes refers to as "Letters" and that we call language. The "door" and "creature" metaphors are poetic, but they may not shed sufficient light. Perhaps another will do. If language is science, as in many aspects it is, then the parts of speech are a shortened version of the periodic table of elements. From them and from the combinations of them, language emerges. The intricacies of the sounds and the symbols we use to understand ourselves, others, and the world become sensible through studying and knowing the parts of speech. If we dismiss them, what we write, what we say, and what we understand from what we read, will remain forever elementary.

The name we have given them is misleading. Calling them "parts of speech" is an insult to the much broader functions they serve. They are as much parts of writing, listening, and reading as parts of speaking. Human language is a beautifully intricate and complex system. One of the many purposes language serves is communication – itself a rich, varied and distinctly human undertaking. It has been claimed that certain animal species can send and receive very limited, very basic message units to each other. However, to suggest that such non-human messaging is akin to human language is little more than anthropomorphic reverie. It is hardly a high commendation of the animal kingdom and it is a particularly resounding insult to human communication. Parts of speech are the opening lesson elements of virtually all language arts textbooks, and with good reason. They specify what function particular sounds accomplish when several sounds are strung together to complete a thought (a sentence).

Even without using the names of the parts of speech, we know and can appreciate the function that particular words serve in a particular succession of words. For example, consider the following simple sentence.

I want food now!

Each of the sound units (words) serves a distinctly different purpose. Parts of speech are merely other words that allow us to identify and qualify those words' purposes. Without using the names of the parts of speech (at least not yet!), let us look at each unit, not in isolation, but in its relation to the other words in the sentence.

I

In our simple sentence example the word "I" designates the person of the speaker and/or the writer, or, if the sentence is spoken, it alerts a listener to the identity of the voice of the person uttering the sounds.

want

This word denotes the action the speaker intends to perform or desires.

food

This word tells us precisely what will receive the action or desire of the speaker, and

now

explains the period of time the speaker intends or desires the action to occur. Parts of speech are nothing more than words (sounds represented by letters when we write) that specify the practical mechanical function of certain other words that are grouped in order to express ideas (sentences). When we understand the functions of words within sentences we can select from among the thousands of words we know and arrange them in ways to make our intended meanings clear. It is as simple as that – and yet it is not simple at all. If it were, there would be no need to read or to write this book. Do not despair; our aim is to improve, not to perfect.

There are eight parts of speech. The sounds that represent the words that represent the ideas of the functions of these eight so-called "parts of speech" may be uttered by decoding the sounds of the letters in the following units;

NOUN

PRONOUN

ADJECTIVE

VERB

ADVERB

PREPOSITION

CONJUNCTION

INTERJECTION

Each of these eight words designates a particularly identifiable function of each of the words written in sentences. The first of many problems in the study of language arts occurs when we come to realize that a word may be correctly identified as a certain part of speech in one sentence, and be a completely different part of speech in another. Rest assured that as your knowledge of the parts of speech broadens, what appears to be a host of irritating contradictions slowly falls away.

2.1 Nouns

NOUN – a word that names a person, place or thing. There are two (2) varieties of nouns;

Common Nouns name non-specific or general purpose....

Persons (man, woman, musician);
Places (city, country, continent); or
Things (cars, coffee, novels).

Proper Nouns name individual or particular....

Persons (James Madison, Marilyn Monroe, Beethoven);
Places (New York, United States, North America); or
Things (Camaro, Maxwell House, A Tale of Two Cities).

Common nouns are not capitalized; proper nouns are. Believe it or not, the word "noun" is a common noun. This sentence contains two nouns.

2.2 Pronouns

PRONOUN – a word used as a substitute for a noun so that
repeated noun use does not become monotonous.

> He, him or his (pronouns for a male
> person, for example, Tom);
>
> She, her or hers (pronouns for a
> female person, for example , Sue);
>
> There, it, that, (pronouns for a place
> or thing, for examples, the USA).

Other pronouns also used as substitutes for nouns include *I, me,
you, we, us, they, them, my, mine, your, yours, our, ours, myself,
yourself, ourselves, themselves, himself, herself, who, whom,
which, that, and whose.* This sentence has one pronoun in it.

2.3 Adjectives

ADJECTIVE – a word that adds information to a noun or a
pronoun...

> In regard to the size, shape, color, quality, number, or any
> other modification. An adjective may be placed before a
> modified word (a *tall* man) or after a modified word (she is
> *slender*). This short sentence contains two adjectives.

2.4 Verbs

VERB – a word that expresses action or assists another verb to
   express an action.

> The action of a verb may be physical (run), mental (think), or
> it may express a state of existence or being (is, are, was, etc.).
> This sentence contains one verb.

2.5 Adverbs

ADVERB – a word that is used to add information to a verb, an
   adjective, or another adverb.

> Adding to the verb played: The band played *loudly*.
> Adding to the adjective
>   intelligent: She is *extremely* intelligent.
> Adding to the adverb quietly: He spoke *very* quietly.

Many adverbs end in "ly," but not all of them do. This sentence
cautiously contains two very subtle adverbs.

2.6 Prepositions

PREPOSITION – a word that shows the physical relation or
   position between a noun or pronoun and some other word
   in the sentence.

Common prepositions include, but are not limited to, the following words: *above, across, beside, below, toward, beyond, upon, over, within, under, past, through and beneath.* This sentence contains one preposition that is cunningly hidden between the words.

2.7 Conjunctions

CONJUNCTION – a word that joins two words (eg. *and, but, or, nor, for*) and pairs of words that join groups of words (eg. *either....or, neither....nor, not only,....but*).

This sentence contains words, phrases, and of course, one example of a conjunction.

2.8 Interjections

INTERJECTION – a single word or phrase that expresses a strong emotion and stands alone from the other words in a sentence.

After thinking long and hard, the author finally composed a sentence that contained an interjection. Great job!

***

Chapter Two Nutshell

Every written word performs one of eight distinct functions and these are known as the parts of speech. Even the eight parts of speech themselves are one of the parts of speech; they are nouns. The eight parts of speech are the eight wonders of the grammatical world. Once you have been exposed to them and understand the power and significance they possess, your world of communication will be transformed.

Chapter Two Exercise

Visit your local library or go online to your favorite search engine and access a copy of the short story "The Necklace," by author Guy de Maupassant. Read the selection and compose an essay not exceeding 100 words that discusses the element of irony in the story. If you are unfamiliar with irony as a literary element, research it, then proceed to write the essay. Do not use any direct quotation or paraphrase from any source.

CHAPTER THREE

PARTS OF SENTENCES

Introduction

Now that the chapter on parts of speech has been reviewed, we can move into other areas of English language arts, and these other areas will be wonderfully illuminated by our newly acquired knowledge of the parts of speech.

As explained in the previous chapter, the parts of speech (as they are imprecisely called) reveal the particular functions of words. In order for a word to possess a function, it must usually appear along with other words – words that will give the particular word a context or meaning. As we know from our experience in speaking and writing, when these groups of accumulated words actually express ideas they are called sentences. We speak in sentences all day long. When spoken sentences are well composed, the people we speak to understand us. When we are hurried or uncertain in what we say, the clarity of our sentences suffers and the people listening to us may become confused or distracted. Communicating with our fellow men and fellow women is difficult enough even when the sentences we speak are clear and direct; when our spoken sentences are muddled and poorly constructed, expressing our thoughts becomes all but impossible. Written sentences and spoken sentences are very similar things, with one very important difference: spoken words are extemporaneous and written words are not, or at least they should not be.

Historically, writing has been a deliberate, intellectual act. The recent advent of computer technology has changed us from deliberate writers to spontaneous writers. Spontaneity is a wonderful trait to possess in our relations with others. However, unless we are highly skilled and thoroughly experienced in quickly reducing what we think to the written word, spontaneity is no friend of written expression. I recall with great misgiving the many e-mails and text messages I have sent that failed utterly to say what I wanted to say – that were so completely misunderstood by the receiver, that much explaining (and occasionally some apologizing) was necessary to make my original meaning clear.

Speed and spontaneity are important elements of modern electronic communication, but they seldom support clarity.

Understanding word function (parts of speech) and appreciating how the functions of words combine to form ideas in sentences is the base-line foundation for writing that cannot be misunderstood. The writing you will be asked to produce as a college graduate is the writing of careful deliberate thought; anyone can dash off a hasty e-mail or respond to a text while sauntering down a busy sidewalk, but good writing demands much more attention.

3.1 Essential Sentence Elements

A correctly written sentence *must* contain two (2) essential elements. Many good sentences contain three (3) elements, but at least two of the possible three (3) must be present in a sentence to do what a sentence is designed to do, and that is to complete a thought. If one or both of the two (2) essential elements are missing, the group of words does not rise to the level of being a sentence. It fails in its attempt to be a sentence because it cannot communicate a complete thought to the reader.

A very popular term used in business and professional meetings today is the "takeaway." The meaning of the word "takeaway" is cleverly lodged in the meanings of the two parts of this compound word. The word means that of all the flood of data presented at a meeting, there are only a few pieces of important information that people attending the meeting should "takeaway" with them at the meeting's end. "Takeaways" can be a helpful tool when studying Standard English grammar. The "takeaway" for this chapter is that correctly written sentences must contain two elements, a subject and a predicate. Once these elements are known and understood by the student, the problems of writing flawed, incorrect sentences will be avoided forever.

The two (2) essential elements of a correctly written sentence are contained in the words "subject" and "predicate." As you may notice, the words "subject" and "predicate" are not contained in the list of terms in the chapter on parts of speech. This is because parts of speech and parts of sentences differ. Parts of speech are the names given to single words within sentences, and parts of sentences can be either single words or groups of related words that combine to serve the purpose of being either a subject or a predicate. Without a subject and a predicate, an attempted sentence cannot serve its essential purpose to complete a thought. A third optional and yet very common element of a sentence is the complement. Complements will be discussed once the student has their "intellectual arms" around the form and substance of the essential elements, the subject and the predicate.

3.2 Subject and Predicate

The subject of a sentence is precisely what the word subject suggests. It is the word or group of words about which the sentence offers its information. The complete subject of the first sentence in this paragraph is "The subject of a sentence," because the subject of a sentence is what the sentence is providing information about. The complete predicate of the first sentence in this paragraph is "...is precisely what the word subject suggests," because the predicate offers or adds information about the subject. Some simpler examples may be called for.

The Subject	**The Predicate**
(essential to a sentence)	(essential to a sentence)
Joseph and Angelina	laughed.
The study of grammar	is challenging.
Studying hard	will be worthwhile.

In terms of parts of speech, each example of the subject contains a noun, nouns, or a noun form, and the predicate contains some form of a verb. The examples are simple, uncomplicated sentences. The more complex a sentence becomes, the more difficult it becomes to accurately identify the subject and the predicate. However, despite the complexity, the subject is always the word or words about which the sentence is offering information, and the predicate is always the word or words that comment about, qualify, act upon, or in some way affect the subject. Neither the simplicity nor the complexity of a sentence changes this relationship of subject to predicate – the subject is always the element discussed, and the predicate is always that which affects the subject.

The interdependency of subject and predicate is immutable. Without providing a discernable subject and attaching an affective predicate a complete thought cannot be expressed and the attempt to write a sentence fails. As proof of this axiom, simply revisit the three short examples of sentences above and read the subject or the predicate in isolation; the words are immediately meaningless. Combining words to express a complete thought demands the appearance of both a subject and a predicate. This is not merely a grammatical rule; it is the most elementary rule of reason.

3.3 Complements

The third part of a sentence is known as the complement. Unlike subjects and predicates, complements are optional, not essential parts of sentences. Nevertheless, complements occur in large numbers of sentences, especially where the idea expressed in the sentence is extensive or complex. As you can imagine, subjects, predicates, and complements can and do occur in countless intricate variations within sentences. For our purposes, and staying true to the spirit of the first word in the title of this book, complements are words that help to "complete" the meaning of a sentence. There are four types of complements; two of them help to complete the meanings of subjects, and two of them help to complete the meanings of predicates. A sentence can be complete and clear without a complement. However, complements can provide additional meaning. They can modify, or qualify the information the sentence offers. A few examples of complements are in the sentences below.

Subject	Predicate	Complement
(essential)	(essential)	(not essential)
John	ran	to the store.
Geometry	is a difficult subject	for students.
Ice skating	builds muscle	in the legs

Understanding the three parts of sentences (especially the two essential parts of subject and predicate) allows a writer to clearly express his or her ideas. Possessing a brilliant mind capable of dazzling calculation and glittering analysis is of very little value if not coupled with the skills to communicate the illumination to others through clear language. In writing and speaking, clarity of expression is paramount. Brilliant thoughts reduced to words and written into sentences that are muddled, clouded, and vague are less than worthless things.

***

Chapter Three Nutshell

Every sentence must contain a subject, a predicate, and complete a thought. The absence of any of these three parts prevents any group of words from being a sentence. Groups of words that fail to rise to the level of a complete sentence will seldom be noticed by a writer in the heat of composition. Revisiting the written text and carefully proofreading it will insure discovery of the problems of failed sentences.

Chapter Three Exercise

Visit your local library or go online to your favorite search engine and access a copy of the poem "Sonnet # 10" (*Death Be Not Proud*) by English poet John Donne. Read the selection and compose an essay not exceeding 100 words that discusses the unusual tone of the poem. If you are unfamiliar with tone as a literary element, research it, then proceed to write the essay. Do not use any direct quotation or paraphrase from any source.

PHRASES

Introduction

As infants, we each begin our life-long study of language arts as a *tabula rasa* (clean slate). Then, as children, after hearing, and endlessly repeating sounds, we slowly acquire the thousands upon thousands of words we eventually have at our disposal to express ourselves. In school we learn that a certain number of those words (eight to be precise) give names to the functions performed by all the words we know and use. We call these parts of speech, though as we have said above, they are parts of much more than just speech. With our thousands of words well in hand, and with the parts of speech in one pocket and the parts of sentences in another, we move toward, or at least move closer toward, an understanding of what happens when we combine certain words. Of course we have been combining words in certain ways in this very paragraph and you have been reading them and understanding them quite well. Here is the irony of language again; if you can read the words in this paragraph (as apparently you are doing at this moment) why do you need to "understand" more than you now know? The answer is not philosophical, it is concrete. If the words you have in hand did not number in the tens of thousands – if they were only a hundred or only a few dozen – you would not need to know very much more. But the tens of thousands of words we have available to express ourselves allow us to make very subtle, or very precise, or even very beautiful combinations of ideas.

In the previous chapter we learned that when we combine words and the combination expresses a complete thought, we have constructed a sentence. When we combine words and the combination does not express a complete though we have usually constructed a phrase. Consider the following combination of words:

John ran across the street.

This combination of words creates a sentence because it expresses a complete thought. The combination

....across the street

does not complete a thought. "Who is across the street," we may ask. "What happened across the street?" This combination of words leaves us with nothing but questions. It is not a sentence, it is a phrase. You have read Chapter Three. You know that "across the street" is not a sentence because it does not complete a thought. You know it does not complete a thought because it does not contain a subject and a predicate. The need for a sentence to contain a subject and predicate is not some arcane artificial rule. It is a simple rule of common sense and reason. Without a subject (a word or words upon which we focus our attention), and without a predicate (a word or words that affect in some way that subject), our mind has insufficient data with which to form a completed thought.

4.1 Phrases

Phrases are groups of words that do not contain a subject or a predicate or both. Phrases are not sentences, but that does not mean they are second class citizens – by no means. Phrases serve very useful purposes. Much of the subtlety, precision, and beauty in our very richly expressive language is the result of the careful insertion of phrases. Without them, many of our sentences would be un-enduringly conventional.

Consider for a moment the word "phrasing" in the field of music. Phrasing in music is the application of certain dynamics to a melodic line – dynamics such as holding a note just a bit longer or ending it just a bit sooner than the note is written, slightly increasing or decreasing volume, or applying a softer or harsher tone in voice or instrument. Musicians and singers apply artistic "phrasing" to add color and texture and emotion to the conventional quarter notes and half notes of a page of music. In much the same way, the groups of words we refer to as phrases can give our writing color, texture and emotion. Phrases may not contain the precious subjects or predicates of our sentences, but they can add detail, clarity, emotion, and drama to our writing.

Although phrases are groups of words, they usually function as a single part of speech. I know what you may be thinking. Parts of speech are the functions of individual words, and phrases are groups of words. Well, how the heck can groups of word function as individual words? I realize the terms "prepositional phrase" and "verbal phrase" may sound like contradictions of terms, but they are not. Prepositional phrases are groups of words that act as a single preposition, and verbal phrases are groups of words derived from verb forms that may act as other single parts of speech. If you find these developments unsettling, make still your heart. These are just a few of the many complexities of English grammar. The exacting study of all the complexities is not for the faint of heart, and is not a prerequisite for acquiring palpable writing skill. For our purposes, know that prepositional phrases are groups of words that show direction or placement, and that verbal phrases are groups of words serving various parts of speech functions.

Examples of three prepositional phrases (and one conjunction) are found in the lines of the beloved holiday song below:

"Over the river and through the woods, to grandmother's house..."

There is no subject and no predicate, just three prepositional phrases. The subject and predicate are cunningly held until the last words of the line.

"we (subject) go (predicate)."

Examples of verbal phrases become a bit more complicated. There are three variations of verbal phrases: the infinitive phrase (which contains a verb form preceded by the word "to" as in the phrase "to conserve," or "to elect"), the participial phrase (which contains a verb form and an auxiliary verb as in the phrase "have stopped," or "am looking"), and the gerund phrase (which contains a verb form that ends in "ing," as in the phrase "running down the hill," or "doing the laundry").

The student will notice that all the examples of phrases above, both prepositional phrases and verbal phrases, are not sentences because they lack subject or predicate or both. The grammatical complexity of phrases is a fascinating study in itself, and may very well attract students into a deeper level of language review. This text is not the resource for that level of study. Ours is a text designed to take conscientious students of writing and, with fundamental instruction, carry them to their highest levels of writing proficiency.

***

Chapter Four Nutshell

Phrases are groups of words that are not sentences because they lack a subject or a verb or both, and function as a single part of speech. The distinction between sentences and phrases is easy to identify. Phrases are only fragments or pieces of thoughts, not complete thoughts. No matter how many phrases are strung together, the result is never a complete thought and never a sentence.

Chapter Four Exercise

Visit your local library or go online to your favorite search engine and access a copy of the play *Hamlet* by William Shakespeare. Turn to Act III, scene iii, lines 36 through 72. A character is speaking to himself. His name is Claudius. He has murdered his brother, stolen what his brother had, and now wants God to forgive him. He raises an interesting moral question. Read the selection and compose an essay not exceeding 100 words that discusses the interesting moral question Claudius raises. Do not use any direct quotation or paraphrase from any source.

CLAUSES

The word "clause" occurs most commonly in writings and discussions of legal matters and contracts. The "penalty clause," the "right to re-enter clause," the "additional rent clause," and the famous "sanity clause" are all examples of the use of the word in legal terminology. In grammatical terms the word "clause" is defined as a group of words (just like a phrase) that contains a subject and a predicate (just like a sentence). At this point a reader may reasonably believe that clauses are sentences. Unfortunately, that student would only be half correct. The annoying irregularities of grammatical terminology and definitions seldom miss an opportunity to mystify the student of grammar, and the definition of the clause is no exception. Yes, a clause contains both a subject and a verb, but no, clauses are not always sentences. Sometimes they are, and sometimes they are not. Fortunately the difference between clauses that are sentences and those that are not sentences is not too hard to spot. Before we explain the distinctions more fully, a few more words of introduction may be helpful.

5.1 Clauses

The study of clauses is often the point at which a writing student comes to the disquieting realization that grammar terms overlap. This "terminology overlap" can be maddening. Take for example the definitions for the phrase and the clause. As noted above, sentences and phrases and clauses all claim to be groups of words. If this is true (and it is), how can a serious-minded student be expected to make sense of it all. Sentences are groups of words! Phrases are groups of words! Clauses are groups of words! Words, words, words – what's to do with all these words? If you have recently arrived at such a point of maddening distress in your studies you may take solace in knowing that you share a special bond with virtually all serious students of language arts. Even students who will not admit to experiencing any such distress, are distressed secretly. Let us proceed with a frank admission that conflicting information conflicts us, but that proceeding in spite of conflict is a personal victory of significant proportion. Knowing that there is sense to be made of all this, and knowing that you will not relent until that sense is made, is a very healthy approach to grammar study and to the study of virtually every other unknown thing.

Clauses are groups of words that contain a subject and a predicate. Alas, the difference between the phrase and the clause is now clearly apparent. Phrases lack a subject and or a predicate, and clauses have both. This is glass clear, and so we move forward. From the chapter on the parts of sentences, we learned that sentences are also groups of words with a subject and a predicate. Therefore, it would seem to follow that clauses are sentences, but as noted above, language study has a way of throwing the proverbial wrench into its own works.

The fact is that some clauses are sentences and some are not. All clauses contain a subject and a predicate, but only some clauses complete a thought, and as you may recall, to be a sentence, a group of words must contain a subject, a predicate, *and complete a thought* (italics added). Without communicating a complete a thought, a group of words containing both a subject and a predicate does not rise to the occasion of being a sentence. To further complicate matters, clauses are of two varieties. Clauses that complete a thought are known as independent or main clauses, and clauses that do not complete a thought are known as dependent or subordinate clauses. For our purposes – purposes which include providing the fundamental grammar with which students can improve their writing – we will refer to the two varieties of clauses as "independent" (can stand alone as sentences), and "dependent" (cannot stand alone as sentences).

5.2 Independent (Main) Clauses

Forgive the repetition, but independent clauses carry the adjective "independent" because they can stand alone as a sentence, and dependent clauses cannot. Dependent clauses need to rely upon or lean on additional words in order to become sentences, thus their words "depend" on the added appearance of other words. Certainly these kinds of distinctions are clear enough, and the modifiers "independent" and "dependent" are sufficiently self-explanatory.

Would it be fair to say that an independent clause is a sentence? Would it be fair to say the terms "independent clause" and "sentence" are interchangeable entities? Yes, it would be fair to say so. If the terms "independent clause" and "sentence" are completely interchangeable, as they are, why do we need two different terms? The answer to that question will become clear when we proceed later in the text to the chapter on sentence types. The importance of being able to distinguish between a sentence and an independent clause will be made clear there. For the present time, our discussion of the independent clause – a group of words that contains a subject and a predicate and completes a thought – are very agreeably at an end.

5.3 Dependent (Subordinate) Clauses

The dependent clause is another matter altogether. You may be asking yourself, how can a group of words contain a subject and a predicate and not complete a thought. That is a well-considered and very reasonable question. The answer, however, may be a little irritating. Dependent clauses do not fail to be sentences because they happen to be missing something they need; they fail to be sentences because they have something extra they do not need. We will call these "extras" qualifying words, but they are also known as subordinating conjunctions. When you have one of these qualifying words (four are shown below, but there are a dozen or more) and you add an independent clause to it, you create a dependent clause. A few examples will be helpful:

Qual. Word   +   *Ind. Clause*   =   *Dep. Clause*

When   John returned from the store...
Unless   the water runs under the bridge....
Before   the president signed the bill......
If   all Linda's homework was completed....

When you read through the four (4) groups of words listed above beginning with the qualifying word listed in the left column, you are reading examples of dependent clauses. As the examples illustrate, a qualifying word plus an independent clause, equals a dependent clause. Read through the examples slowly. You will notice how the qualifying words transform the otherwise independent clause (a sentence in its own right) into a dependent clause that does not complete a thought. When we read the words, "John returned from the store," we have a perfectly valid sentence or independent clause. However, when we qualify that group of words by inserting "When" as the beginning word, the entire word group loses its character as a sentence because the thought is left mysteriously incomplete. What happened when John returned from the store? We do not know. If the water does not run under the bridge, what will occur? We have no idea. What took place before the president signed the bill? It is anyone's guess. We do not know these things so the thought attempted to be expressed by the group of words is incomplete and no sentence results. When a group of words purports to answer a question but does not, the words do not constitute a sentence. Once again, this is not a rule for rules' sake, it is a rule of common sense, reason, and logic.

If dependent clauses are not sentences because they fail to complete a thought, what purpose do they serve? If we leave them in their pitiable state of incompleteness, dependent clauses serve no purpose – they are useless. However, when they are properly attached to an independent clause they can become a very efficient, very effective thought-completing machine. Proper attachment of a dependent clause to an independent clause, or of an independent clause to a dependent clause (the order is immaterial) creates a sentence that can express a complex thought with surprising clarity. That proper attachment will be explained in all its beauty and in the proceeding chapter on sentence types. Stay tuned.

***

Chapter Five Nutshell

A clause is a group of words that contains a subject and a predicate and may stand alone as a sentence (an independent clause) or may not stand alone and is not a sentence (dependent clause). Independent clauses complete a thought; dependent clauses do not complete a thought.

Chapter Five Exercise

Visit your local library or go online to your favorite search engine and access a copy of the essay entitled "Meditation upon a Broomstick" by Jonathan Swift. Carefully read the essay and determine what Swift is thinking. Compose an essay not exceeding 100 words that explains the curious analogy that Swift is making in the essay. Do not use direct quotation or paraphrase from any source.

CHAPTER SIX

SENTENCE STRUCTURES AND SENTENCE TYPES

Introduction

In our first five chapters we have been exposed to a substantial portion of the "ground work" of grammar studies. This exposure should have instilled at least a passing familiarity with the eight parts of speech, the three elements necessary in the formation of sentences, the two basic forms of phrase word groups, the two basic forms of clause word groups, and the distinctions between phrases and clauses. These preliminary studies have presented us with some of the very basic and fundamental substructures of language arts. They are precisely the studies that will support our primary objective of improving student writing. The present chapter and those following it will continue this pursuit of presenting technical information designed to positively affect compositional skill. However, a few words of caution may be called for.

Mere knowledge of rules and principles does not an accomplished writer make...not necessarily. Writing is not merely a static "rule-driven" manipulation of words. When done well, writing uses rules to best accomplish the work at hand. Rules, principles, and axioms do not drive the writing process, they guide it. Knowing them and understanding them is the base-line for producing good writing, but while they may be the bricks and mortar, they do not guarantee a sound building. Solidly structured writing also depends on design and style, two elements that will be carefully reviewed in later chapters of the text. For now, we dutifully return to our study of the bricks and mortar.

The subtle differences between writing rules and writing style discussed in the preceding paragraph are noticeable to some extent in this chapter on sentences. There are sentence structures and sentence types. Sentence structures are akin to the physical forms of sentences – the moving parts the sentences use to do the job of expressing thoughts that range from very uncomplicated to very complicated ideas. Sentence types, unlike the more physical forms found in sentence structures, are best thought of as the designs or the styles of sentences. It may be helpful to think of structures as the concrete parts of sentences and types are the creative parts. If these kinds of distinctions are getting a bit too ephemeral for the student, simply pack them away for now. Perhaps a later discussion will clear the clouds.

There are four (4) sentence structures. They are the simple, the compound, the complex, and the compound-complex. These four structures are listed here in their order of intricacy from the least intricate to the most intricate. When we write we should select sentence structures that best express the intricacy level of the ideas we intend to convey. Many writers disregard the importance of selecting the proper sentence structure. If clarity of expression is the foremost aim in all our writing – and it most certainly is – and if selecting an effective structure for expressing a particular idea will aid clarity, then failing to do so is almost criminal. Conversely, selecting the proper structure deserves commendation. A sentence structure should be selected that comports with the level of intricacy that the sentence's idea calls for. Learning to make the proper selection is a burden; once learned, the process becomes second nature, and the writer's writing is improved exponentially.

6.1. Four Sentence Structures

6.1.1 The Simple Sentence

The simple sentence structure contains one independent clause. As you may recall from your understanding of Chapter Five, an independent clause is a group of words that has a subject, a predicate, and completes a thought; simple is as simple does. This is not to say that all simple sentences express uncomplicated ideas. Many contain ideas that are thoroughly intricate; it is the structure of the simple sentence that is straightforward and uncomplicated. However, for the purposes of example we will present simple sentences that contain simple ideas. Consider the following simple sentence:

Maurice left the room.

As you know, "Maurice" is the subject and "left the room" is the predicate. It is a simple sentence structure because it contains one independent clause. You may be asking yourself, when exactly does an independent clause become a sentence? The answer is an independent clause becomes a sentence at the exact moment a period is placed at the end of the group of words.

Every teacher who has had to undertake the reading of stacks of student papers will wholeheartedly agree that short, simple sentences are beautiful things. College students seem to disagree. Many undergraduates prefer to write in the more complicated sentence structures, and when they do, grammatical corruption is almost sure to follow. Phrases, clauses, conjunctions, and commas clutter the page willy-nilly until whatever idea was intended becomes shrouded in mystery.

Strangely enough (and it is a strangeness I have never understood) many students believe that writing a sentence whose meaning is mysterious is the true badge of possessing higher education. The more confusion and obfuscation a sentence can create, the greater the proof of high intellect. With very few exceptions, this student creed is universal and indestructible. Allow me to offer the single most important writing rule for all student writers of all educational levels: simple is best. Simplicity serves clarity, and clarity is the primary objective of the written word.

At this point, students are often quick to point out the structural complexity of a Charles Dickens novel and the flabbergasting grammatical gymnastics of the great poets. We will address these issues in later chapters. For now, the conscientious student should keep in mind that he or she is not writing novels or poems, at least not yet. Term papers, examinations, reports, and writing samples generally call for clarity, not creative flair. The earlier declaration bears repeating; short, simple sentences are beautiful things.

6.1.2 The Compound Sentence

The compound sentence structure consists of two simple sentences properly joined. Perhaps a more accurate statement would be that the compound sentence structure is the proper joining of two independent clauses. The very name of the structure (compound) supports this rather obvious explication. There are two ways to properly join two independent clauses and thereby form a compound sentence.

The first way is to insert a correctly placed comma and an appropriate conjunction after the first clause and place a period at the end of the second. A conjunction is one of the venerable parts of speech visited in Chapter Two. That chapter will refresh your recollection as to what a conjunction is if you need to have your recollection refreshed. The comma and period will be reviewed in a later chapter. An example of a compound sentence is below:

Maurice left the room, and Mr. Perkins closed the door.

The second way to form a compound sentence structure is to place a semicolon at the end of the first independent clause and a period at the end of the second. An example of this method of formation is seen below:

Maurice left the room; Mr. Perkins closed the door.

As you may have noticed from the examples, both the first and the second methods of forming the compound sentence structure are strikingly similar. Yes, the similarity is striking, and the difference is very slight, but the difference, however slight to the eye, is a big difference in tone.

These two methods of forming a compound sentence are a perfect example of the very subtle distinctions our language is capable of making. In the first formation where the conjunction is used, Maurice leaving and Mr. Perkins closing the door are presented as merely two actions, one followed by the other. In the second formation, the absence of the conjunction removes the separation between the two actions. The semicolon connects them. The second is now somehow bonded or related to the first. The reader gets a sense that leaving the room and closing the door are somehow interrelated. The difference is subtle indeed, but the feeling of connection between the actions lingers in the second formation.

Use of the semicolon to connect two independent clauses to form a compound sentence structure carries with it that vague hint of connection between the ideas in the clauses. When no such connection is intended, the first formation (comma and conjunction) should be used.

6.1.3 The Complex Sentence

The complex sentence structure is a bit more....complex. It consists of the proper combining of one independent clause and one dependent clause. As you know from your study of Chapter Five both the independent clause and the dependent clause contain subjects and predicates. The independent clause is so called because it completes a thought and can stand alone as a sentence in its own right. The dependent clause does not complete a thought because it contains an added "qualifying" word that raises a question that is not answered. This unanswered question interrupts completion of the thought and makes the clause dependent. When a dependent clause is correctly attached to an independent clause, the unanswered question is addressed and the thought is rendered complete. The correct attachment of independent and dependent clauses results in the formation of a complex sentence structure. In the examples below the qualifying words of the dependent clauses are in italics.

INDEPENDENT CLAUSE

DEPENDENT CLAUSE

The sound of the wheels was muffled

when the train entered the tunnel.

Patricia scribbled out a hasty note
> *after* the manager turned toward her desk.

The bill could not be paid
> *unless* the money fell from the sky.

Color blazed across the horizon
> *where* the clouds defused the setting sun.

As the examples above illustrate, both the independent and dependent clauses have subjects and predicates, but the qualifying words of the dependent clauses interrupt the complete thought and the dependent clause cannot stand alone as a sentence. Read the dependent clauses alone – they do not make sense. Omit the qualifying word from a dependent clause and you have a valid independent clause, but add the qualifier, and completion of the thought fails. Properly attaching a dependent clause with qualifier to an independent clause solves the failure to complete the thought. The result is a clearly understandable "complex" sentence.

6.1.4 The Compound-Complex Sentence

Finally there is the Compound-Complex sentence structure. This structure bears the same relation to the complex sentence as the compound sentence bears relation to the simple sentence. Namely, a compound-complex sentence is one that contains a compound sentence and a complex sentence. Kindly excuse what may seem to many as endless repetition, but as mentioned earlier regarding memorization, repetition of ideas that is structured and disciplined is a time-tested friend of learning. Just think back upon the many things our mothers repeated to us and how those words of wisdom are forever burned into us. To continue, compound-complex sentence structures contain at least two independent clauses (compound) and at least one dependent clause (complex). Examples are provided below, and the qualifying word of the dependent clause is in italics.

TWO INDEPENDENT CLAUSES

                              ONE DEPENDENT CLAUSE

John began to chuckle, and Mary laughed aloud

                              when the clown fell off the chair.

Math is difficult, and science is baffling

                              if students do not apply themselves.

The party was cancelled; Diane was heartbroken

                              because the party would have been fun.

The accomplished student writer will make a habit of varying the sentence structures they use in composition. The simple, the compound, the complex, and the compound-complex structures will be employed as they may best suit exposition of the material at hand. There is no need to use them all, and no need to use them in any order or number. They are available to meet the writer's needs and to serve the purposes of clarity for the reader. As with all the details of all the materials in all the chapters, the writer must use sentence structure selection in ways that take careful aim at and strike the mark of clarity.

6.2 Four Sentence Types

Sentence types (unlike sentence structures) have to do with the information and content of a sentence, not with its grammatical elements. A writer selects a particular sentence type so that the material in the sentence will be presented in a proper framework and context. Sentence structures have to do with the formation of a sentence idea; sentence types have more to do with the content of the idea. Both sentence structure and sentence type should be chosen carefully by the writer to insure clarity and maintain reader interest. Monotonous repetition of the same sentence structure and the same sentence type in any paragraph is a gilded invitation to reader boredom.

There are four sentence types: the declarative sentence, the imperative sentence, the interrogative sentence, and the exclamatory sentence. As with sentence structures, sentence types should be used interchangeably to best express the ideas communicated in the writing. Along with careful attention to all the suggestions in previous chapters, the appropriate variation of sentence types (and structures) will keep a reader interested.

6.2.1 The Declarative Sentence

The declarative sentence states facts or makes a .....declaration. In its simplest form it is direct and unambiguous. Standing alone, a declarative sentence does not lead to a conclusion or seek to defend or promote a position. It states information or data in much the same way as the account of an historical event or the details of a business report. An example of a declarative sentence follows:

Thirty-nine votes
were counted before the chairperson announced
that the motion had carried.

6.2.2 The Imperative Sentence

The imperative uses what is commonly referred to as the command form. This sentence form ordinarily does away with the subject because the subject is presumed to be the singular pronoun "you." Imperative sentences usually express a short, insistent order to act or move. They often appear to be predicates hanging in thin air without a subject. However, because the subject "you" is presumed, the group of words is in fact a complete sentence in spite of the absence of a visible, printed subject. Imperative sentences are the favorites of exasperated parents and other persons in authority. Three examples of imperative sentences are provided below:

Close that door.
Step away from the vehicle.
Stop annoying your brother.

6.2.3 The Interrogative Sentence

The interrogative sentence asks a question and is always followed by a question mark rather than a period. Occasionally the injection of a question into series of sentences can peak the reader's interest in ways that standard sentence types cannot. A rhetorical question – a question whose answer is presumed to be understood – can be an effective writing tool. Properly placed, the interrogative sentence can invigorate a paragraph. A sample interrogative sentence appears below:

Will anyone deny that
the New York Rangers
are the greatest hockey players in the world?

6.2.4 The Exclamatory Sentence

The exclamatory sentence expresses emotion and it is always followed by an exclamation point rather than a period. If the group of words in a sentence is not presented with high emotion, it is not an appropriate exclamatory sentence. Usually exclamatory sentences occur in direct address as when someone speaks excitedly. An example of the exclamatory sentence follows:

We must stop the violence now!

In the succeeding chapters there will be additional discussion on developing the skill of selecting proper sentence structures and sentence types. As mentioned above, learning to write well (as learning to do most anything well) always begins with slowly acquiring basic skills. Sentence selection is such a skill and the acquisition is a slow go, not unlike the skills acquired by seasoned professional athletes. However, once in hand, it will become as effortless and as accurate as an NBA fowl shot, an NHL slap shot, or an American League swing for the fences.

***

Chapter Six Nutshell

There are four sentence structures and four sentence types. Knowing all structures and all types allows a writer to vary sentence construction and adapt sentences to the purposes they serve. Do not condemn your writing to monotony. Vary your sentences.

Chapter Six Exercise

Visit your local library or go online to your favorite search engine and access a copy of the sonnet entitled "Piano After War" by Gwendolyn Brooks. Carefully read the poem over several times. Move over the words slowly and keep a careful eye on the punctuation signals. Then compose an essay not exceeding 100 words that discusses the sad incongruity of the Brooks' lyric. Do not use direct quotation or paraphrase from any source.

CHAPTER SEVEN

SENTENCE PROBLEMS

7.1 On the Need to Proofread

As you have certainly noticed by now, this book is chock full of good advice for writers. The single most important piece of advice in the book – the advice that will have the most dramatic effect on the quality of student writing – is to carefully proofread what you have written. Without proofreading, memorizing every rule printed in every volume of every grammar book is pointless.

Sentence problems will never come to light unless the sentence writer discovers them, and they will never be discovered unless the writer reads what has been written.

Of course, the opportunity to proofread is not always available. There are times when we must dash off a short message, or write an extended piece within a restricted time frame such as notetaking, writing an essay-style examination, or preparing a writing sample during a job interview. These kinds of writings are not afforded the luxury of proofreading and revision. When time constraints will not permit us to review our writing we must rely upon the good writing habits we have developed to carry us through. However, for all those other times – times when we are writing reports, affidavits, supporting papers, explanations, formal letters, recommendations, speeches, and all the other writing pieces that will become part of our jobs as college educated persons – we must write and then proofread and then revise. For every writer, even those whose writing is only occasional, the three step process of write, proof, and revise needs to become as habitual as good grooming.

Informal speaking has to be extemporaneous, and short-burst writing of notes, e-mails, and text messages are usually spontaneous things, but formal writing designed to be formally presented to a discerning readership must be neither spontaneous nor extemporaneous – it must be written, proofread, and revised.

In that tradition of formality, this chapter will identify the several most common sentence problems, and provide instruction on how to correct them. Correction depends entirely upon discovery and, as stated above, discovery will never come to light without a thorough and meticulous proofreading. As every writer knows, proofreading is not among the most pleasant of pastimes. When done well, it is a troublesome two-step process. The first step is admitting to ourselves that we are capable of making mistakes (this step is difficult for most of us). The second is actually finding the mistakes (this step is painful for most of us). Proofreading is an easy thing to avoid. We much prefer to believe that our first draft is very nearly perfect. Thus we either avoid proofreading altogether, or we proof cursorily, unconsciously skipping over scores of glaring errors. Proofreading is fraught with trouble first and last. Nevertheless, without it we are condemned to a purgatory of unclear, imprecise, and problem-ridden writing. Proofread!

7.2 Fragments and Run-ons

As noted in an earlier chapter, one of the essential elements of a sentence is the completion of a thought. When we write we are usually anxious to get our thoughts onto screen or paper before we lose them. When thoughts come to us in pieces or in bunches or connected to other thoughts, our writing does its best to sort them out and record them. Despite doing our best however, the thoughts often get broken apart, or jumbled and jostled into amorphous blobs, or stretched out into long ramblings of words that have lost their original connections. These breaks, blobs, stretches, and ramblings are the stuff that sentence fragments and run-on sentences are made of.

A fragment is a sentence that fails because it lacks one or more of the three essential elements; a subject, a predicate, and a thought completed. Another way to describe the fragment is to say it is either a phrase (or a group of phrases) in isolation, or a dependent clause.

Fragments are never sentences because they always lack one or more of the essential elements of a sentence. Don't let the word "fragment" fool you. Yes, fragments may be short, but they may also be as long as "all get out." A few examples of short fragments are below:

The door at the end of the hallway...
Only seventeen overdue books with red covers...
The entire artificial turf playing field....

As you may have noticed, the fragments above are subjects without predicates. They sound interesting perhaps, but they are only pieces of thoughts. If you add predicates to these fragments you can complete the thoughts of the subjects and have valid sentences. Two examples of longer fragments are below:

The only way to stop the advance and put an end to the conflict between the parties who have become such bitter enemies and vowed to destroy one another.........(this is a long, detailed subject without a predicate)

.........to take the initiative, complete all the work that had been promised by the contractor, pay the outstanding bills, and remove all the debris from the site before the inspector arrived....... (this is a long predicate without a subject)

There are lots of words in the examples above, but lots of words do not necessarily a sentence make. The absence of an essential element leaves us with a fragment. Add the missing element and a healthy sentence will emerge.

Run-ons are usually sentences that are of the "bunched ideas" variety. Unlike fragments, run-ons do contain all of the essential sentence elements. The problem is they usually contain too many of them and the result is always confusing for the reader. Instead of being presented with ideas in an understandable sequence, the run-on sentence presents a reader with groups of subjects and predicates that cannot be sorted out. They fall over each other in a tumbling mass of ideas that quickly become unintelligible. Earlier in the book we noted that short sentences are beautiful things, and indeed they are. However, complicated ideas occasionally require longer sentences with multiple phrases and clauses. The trick is to maintain clarity. An example of an unclear run-on sentence follows:

> The elder gentleman spoke quietly with the mayor who was standing beside the door to the conference room where several students gathered to protest the arrival of the governor who had passed the tax abatement bill over the objection of many state legislators, including first term state senator Lucas Bansin who represented the constituents living in the district closest to the university.

A run-on sentence might also be described as too much of a good thing. Yes, there are lots of subjects and predicates and complete ideas in the example above, but they are crowded together in a jumble of related ideas. The reader can sense that there is a point to all the information, but the point is lost because the mass of ideas cannot be sorted out properly.

Run-on sentences can usually be corrected by making two or three sentences out of the one run-on. If the jumble of ideas are logically related to a main idea, then slowly sort out the related ideas and group them in a few shortened, digestible sentences. Sometimes the careful insertion of periods and commas in appropriate places can correct a run-on sentence nicely. Other times, a more resolute re-writing is called for. Preventing or correcting the run-on sentence is not a major production. A good rule of thumb is the "20 word rule." Look at the general length of your sentences. If the number of words exceeds 20, or if a sentence exceeds three printed lines, it may be on the verge of becoming a run-on.

Just as with fragments, run-ons will never be corrected unless they are identified, and identification will never occur without careful proofreading.

7.3 Subject-Verb Agreement

The subject of a sentence, and the verb contained in the predicate of that sentence must agree in number. "Agree in number" means that if the subject of a sentence is singular in number then the verb in the predicate of that sentence must also be singular in number. Please review the examples below (the verbs are in italics):

SINGULAR SUBJECTS	SINGULAR VERBS
John	*runs* to school.
The library	*opens* at nine o'clock.
The necklace	*costs* thousands of dollars.

Similarly, if the subject of a sentence is plural in number the verb of the predicate must also agree in number. "Agree in number" means that if the subject of a sentence is plural in number then the verb in the predicate of the sentences must also be plural in number, as shown below (the verbs are in italics):

PLURAL SUBJECT	PLURAL VERB
John and Mary	*run* to school.
All city libraries	*open* at nine o'clock.
The three necklaces	*cost* thousands of dollars.

If you have read through the examples above you may have noticed an annoying aberration. We often (and quite correctly) associate the formation of the plural form of nouns with the addition of the letter "s." Thus the singular "shoe" becomes shoes, singular "house" becomes houses, and singular "computer" becomes computers. This is one of the appealing simplicities in the complex world of grammatical rules. The aberration is that the general rule for forming the plural of many verbs is just the opposite, which is to remove the final "s." The singular "runs" becomes "run" in the plural, the singular "opens" becomes open, and the singular "costs" becomes cost in plural. A quick review of the charted examples above will point this out dramatically. It is an irritating affront to simplicity, but it is one with which we must learn to live.

In view of this aberration the thoughtful student might suggest that it would be less confusing if the rule were changed to read, "a singular subject takes a plural verb." This may seem well-advised, but then the word "agreement" would be compromised. Therefore, in the interest of simplicity, however complicated simplicity may sometimes become, we must accept the subject-verb singular/singular, plural/plural rule.

The thoughtful student might also raise another interesting point in the matter of subject-verb agreement. It is that verbs, as simple parts of speech in and of themselves, do not really have either "singular-ness" or "plural-ness." Nouns do, but verbs do not. This is quite true. So when we use the term "subject-verb agreement," the words singular and plural only apply to verbs in their relation to the subject nouns with which they must agree. It is an esoteric point, but an interesting one just the same.

If we consider the materials in this chapter so far, subject-verb agreement does not present much of a problem, and since the chapter is entitled "Sentence Problems" we need to move onto matters of subject-verb agreement that are more seriously problematic.

When a subject noun is in close proximity to the verb in the predicate, agreeing the noun with the verb is relatively simple (as shown in the examples above). Unfortunately, many sentences insert several pesky words or phrases in between the noun and the verb, and agreement becomes difficult. Occasionally a rash of non-subject plural nouns can lead us astray from selecting the proper singular form of the verb. Consider the following example:

> The true source of military courage, whether on the fields of battle, beside the crash of canons, or amid the flourish of swords, is (not "are") in the heart.

The simplest and surest way to properly agree a subject and a verb is to find the subject, block out all the words that come between it and the verb, then check to make sure there is agreement. This will insure that intervening words and phrases are not throwing you off the subject-verb agreement track. Avoid the problems of subject-verb agreement and you have avoided one of the top three most common grammatical errors in the English language.

7.4 Pronoun-Antecedent Problems

A quick flip of pages back to Chapter 2 on the Parts of Speech will refresh your recollection that the pronoun is a word that substitutes for a noun. The reason we substitute a pronoun for a noun is to avoid monotony and improve clarity. A pronoun's antecedent is simply a fancy name for the noun that the pronoun is standing in for. The word "antecedent" simply means, that which comes before. In the two sentences below the antecedent and its pronoun are in italics:

ANTECENDENT   PRONOUN

John won the race.   *He* is a strong swimmer.

"John," in the first sentence is the antecedent of the pronoun "He" in the second sentence. Substituting "he" for John, "she" for Mary, "they" for John and Mary, "that" for a word or group of words that describes some thing, "we" for a group to which the writer or speaker belongs, and lots of other pronouns as noun substitutions, helps clarify a writer's meaning and keeps a reader focused.

> *Take a quick look at the last sentence in the above paragraph that begins with the word "Substituting." For a moment, think back to the rule from the previous section, "Subject-Verb Agreement." The subject is "Substituting" (a singular noun form known as a gerund). The two verbs "helps" and "keeps" are correctly written in the singular form. They may not "sound" correct because of the many intervening plural nouns, but they are. Now back to Pronoun-Antecedent!*

When a pronoun is in close proximity to the noun it is substituting, there is usually no problem keeping the relation of pronoun to antecedent clear for the reader. However, when the pronoun and its antecedent are separated by intervening words and phrases, the relation is attenuated and the reader may become confused. This confusion problem is similar to the proximity problem in subject-verb agreement. It can be avoided by placing pronouns as reasonably close to the nouns that are antecedent to them. It is not uncommon for a pronoun and its antecedent to be separated by one or more sentences. This separation is not necessarily a problem if the writer remains sensitive to the reader's need to keep the flow of ideas uninterrupted. A good writer does not stretch the reader's ability to connect the pronoun-antecedent dots.

However, keeping close proximity and clear association between pronouns and their antecedents does not solve all problems. Occasionally a writer needs to place two nouns together that form a plural or "compound" subject, then later uses a singular pronoun that confuses the reader. The example sentences below demonstrate the problem:

> *Silvio and Carlos* are friends and are very much alike. However, everyone knows *he* always does better in school.

The writer of the sentence presumably knows which of the two fellows does better in school, but has inadvertently failed to communicate that fact to the reader. The result is that the antecedent of the pronoun "he" is utterly unclear. Forgive me for harping, but problems such as these (and a plethora of others) are seldom discovered without careful proofreading.

7.5 Logic Problems

Logic-problem sentences can be perfectly grammatical is all other respects. One of the finest examples of a grammatically correct sentence that contains a logic problem is illustrated in the title of a 1969 American comic film.

> If It's Tuesday, This Must Be Belgium.

The idea in the opening clause has no logical relation to the idea in the second clause. Formal logic is a study of extraordinary complexity. In terms of grammar and language study, logic is the formation of understandable connections between successive ideas.

Writers have a primary obligation to make their meanings clear. Providing logical connections between ideas is one important step toward that clarity (along with all the other rules in this chapter and in this book).

Let us return for a moment to our example. What in the name of goodness did the writer of the example sentence/film title mean when he or she wrote, "If it's Tuesday, this must be Belgium"? How are "Tuesday" and "Belgium" connected?

Plainly, without some additional information (presumably from the actual content of the film) a reader of the words of the sentence/title will never know what the connection is. This is a classic logic-problem sentence. The words seem to suggest that the second idea (Belgium) is somehow consequent upon the first idea (Tuesday), but there is no logical connector. This absence baffles the reader, and the sentence fails miserably. If readers of the sentence were to view the film they would discover the underlying "logic." The sentence refers to the bafflingly unpredictable nature of European guided tours, and how tourists caught up in the whirlwind of peripatetic travels can lose all sense of space and time.

The sentence could have been modified into a logical form thus:

> If it's Tuesday, and if the touring schedule we received is accurate, this must be Belgium.

By leaving out one connective piece of information, the two ideas "Tuesday" and "Belgium" become unrelated absurdities; add the connector, and the pieces sequence logically.

Student writers who write in much the same way as they speak, often compose logic-problem sentences. When we speak to others and inadvertently leave out a connecting piece of information, the listener can stop us, ask a question, and we can fill in the missing connector. When we write, the speaker-listener exchange does not exist. Readers have no other source for information than the writer's words on the page. If logic is not maintained, the result is bitter obscurity.

***

Chapter Seven Nutshell

Sentence problems are many and varied and troublesome, but once discovered they are easily corrected. The problem lies in discovery. Sentence problems will never come to light without proofreading. Therefore proofreading is critical to good writing.

Chapter Seven Exercise

Visit your local library or go online to your favorite search engine and access a copy of the collected political essays entitled "The Federalist Papers" co-authored by Alexander Hamilton, James Madison and John Jay. Carefully read the paper entitled "Federalist 10" written by Madison. Compose an essay not exceeding 100 words that discusses what you believe is Madison's controlling theme in the essay. Do not use direct quotation or paraphrase from any source.

CHAPTER EIGHT

PUNCTUATION

8.1 The Purposes of Punctuation

Punctuation is a system of marked, non-letter symbols that are inserted at various points in a unit of writing to elicit specific reader responses intended to assist the reader in understanding what is written. When punctuation marks are properly used, a writer's meaning is strongly assisted; when they are misused or used not at all, the meaning of the written word can be seriously compromised. Punctuation marks are signposts. The signpost metaphor is overused but valid nonetheless. Every mark serves a particular purpose, alerting the traveling reader of what was, what is, or what will be encountered. Every feature in the compositional landscape becomes sharper and clearer when seen through the lens of appropriate punctuation.

This chapter will review and outline eleven of the most common punctuation marks. Some of these are of the indispensable, others of the rare, variety. All in all, they provide a writer with a full box of tools to build sentences that are enduring.

8.2 Eleven Punctuation Marks

8.2.1 The period (.)

The period is one of three marks of end punctuation. The period comes at the end of a sentence and indicates to the reader that the group of words preceding the period contains a subject, a predicate, and a completed thought. If a reader comes to a period and is confused as to what idea has been expressed, the period invites him or her to revisit the words of the sentence for meaning. As the reader here will recall, all declarative sentences end with a period. Stated another way, sentences that end in a period do not ask a question and do not express strong emotion. A writer who fails to place a period at the end of a sentence in a continuing paragraph leads the reader to read straight through to the words of the next complete thought. This very often results in reader confusion. The "signpost" period that should have marked the end of one complete thought, and should have prepared the reader to take up the next one, was not there to do its job. In earlier chapters we have discussed at length the importance of forming sentences that contain the three essentials, and we have reviewed sentence structures and sentence types. It is worth noting that all the work that goes into sentence construction can be wasted for the want of one small round dot.

Once again, and certainly not for the last time before this volume is complete, the importance of proofreading deserves special note. Misplaced or forgotten-to-be-placed periods will continue to inflict pain and suffering upon scores of innocent readers unless writers do their duty and punctuationally proofread what they have written.

8.2.2 The Question Mark (?)

The question mark is the second of the three marks of end punctuation. It is placed at the end of an interrogative sentence. As you are painfully aware from your exhaustive study of the chapter on sentence types, interrogative sentences ask a question. The artistically curved head and straight lower stem of the question mark are distinctive. There is a reason for the distinction. It serves to dazzle and amaze the eye of an unsuspecting reader. It is a mark that does not resemble any other punctuation symbol. It drives home the important point that a sentence that has such a mark at its terminus is....special. The "specialness" is its interrogatory nature; the writer has deliberately posed a question. Whether it is a rhetorical question (the answer is "understood") or a question whose answer the writer wants the reader to consider independently, the question mark tells the reader to take special notice. Writers often underestimate the value of writing interrogative sentences. When a writer goes to the trouble to compose a valuable interrogative sentence he or she should always remember to end-punctuate the sentence with a question mark. I will end this chapter subsection with a rhetorical question. In writing, is there anything more important than clarity?

8.2.3 The Exclamation Point (!)

The exclamation point is the last of the three end punctuation marks, although it is not in anyway last in ranking or importance. Properly placed, all punctuation is equally critical to clear writing. An exclamation point is placed at the end of a sentence that expresses strong emotion. The question is begged, "so what exactly constitutes strong emotion?" The answer is that strong emotion is a judgement call within the discretion of the writer. However, that discretion should not be abused. A writer that over-uses the exclamation point to end-punctuate sentences that are not expressing sincerely strong emotion, will annoy the reader. Over-use will blunt a reader's sensibility to what is truly emotional. The sentence example below may be helpful in exercising exclamation point discretion:

Unprovoked terrorist activity must be stopped!

The use of an exclamation point in the sentence above may be appropriate or it may not. If the writer of the sentence is calmly discussing international affairs, a period as end punctuation may be perfectly acceptable. On the other hand, if the writer is dashing off a fiery editorial in the wake of an international incident, use of the exclamation point can be defended. In any event, the exclamation point should be used sparingly so that when it is employed, it carries weight.

8.2.4 The Comma (,)

If frequency of use is the measure of a punctuation mark, the comma is the undisputed king of punctuation. A comma is an internal, not an end-punctuation mark. The period tells a reader when to come to a complete stop; the comma indicates a pause. It is as simple as that. Countless rules apply to the proper use of the comma, but virtually all of them can be reduced to one: the comma serves the purpose of reading clarity. When a gentle pause between words in a sentence will demonstrably clarify sentence meaning, then a comma is called for. When the clarity purpose is not served, forego the comma and keep writing. When the comma is overused, the meaning of a sentence can become unclear. One example can be found in the sentence immediately preceding this one that begins with the word, "When...." Is that sentence properly punctuated? It has end punctuation as it must, and as we know, end punctuation is not discretionary – it is essential. What about the comma after the word "overused"?

When the comma is overused, the meaning of a sentence can become unclear. The opening group of words, "When the comma is overused," is a dependent clause and the words following it are the main or independent clause. It is a complex sentence. Should a comma always appear between the dependent and independent clauses of a complex sentence? The answer is no, it should not always appear, but it may if it adds to clarity.

Here we are at another grammatical crossroad. Shall we turn onto the path crowded with long lists of comma rules and begin citing them all, each with its illustrating examples, or shall we move through the intersection and briefly explain the general rationale that underlies each and every comma rule? I think the relative thinness of this volume gives you the answer. All commas, from those that place a subtle pause between sentence parts (phrases, and clauses) to those that set apart the individual words or items in lists, all serve the purpose of clarity.

A student writer may not have yet achieved the writing instinct for the proper use of the comma, but it is an instinct and it is learned over the course of writing time. How is it learned without a thorough exposure to each and every comma rule? It is learned by listening to and hearing the cadence of the sentences you write. If the comma is a signpost indicating a pause in the flow of words, then it is a thing to be heard, not a thing to be known. Proofread what you have written and listen to the ebb and flow of your words. The natural pauses will naturally present themselves; the artificial ones will sound awkward and out of place. Insert commas to accommodate the naturals, and eliminate them from the artificials. Do this well, and chances are the litany of comma rules can remain forever unstudied.

8.2.5 The Colon (:)

The colon is a mark resembling two periods stacked vertically one above the other. Aside from its grammatical uses, it plays a humiliating part in the construction of the emoji, a set of two annoyingly pretentious symbols used to close e-mails and text messages. If viewed sideways, the colon, along with its accompanying open or closed single parenthesis, appears as either a smiling or a frowning face. The colon is the "eyes" and the parenthesis is the "mouth." An example is below:

:) – smiling

:(– frowning

Such use of the colon and the single parenthesis is a frivolous affectation and a punctuational affront. Students should avoid such a disrespectful exploitation of these two otherwise honorable marks of punctuation.

The colon's appropriate use is to stop a reader. This may sound similar to the use of the period and the other end punctuation marks in general, but the colon is distinguishable. The colon stops the reader, then signals them that what immediately follows is of a special character. Upon seeing the colon, readers should prepare themselves for the subsequent presentation of information that is in a special format.

The colon has two conventional uses. It can introduce a list of data items, or it can appear at the end of the salutation portion in a business letter. A colon does not appear at the end of the salutation in a friendly letter, only at the salutation end in the business letter. These two uses are outlined in the examples set forth below:

LIST OF ITEMS
There are eight parts of speech: noun, pronoun, verb, adjective, adverb, preposition, conjunction, and interjection.

BUSINESS LETTER SALUTATION
Dear Superintendent Smith:
Dear President Morales:

Colons and semi colons are as easy to mistake for one another as periods and commas. However, like periods and commas, colons and semi colons are very much unalike in both form and function. Semi colons will be discussed hereinbelow.

8.2.6 Semicolons (;)

The semicolon is a punctuation mark containing a period that is stacked vertically above a comma. It is no accident that the two marks appear together. The period in the semicolon tells a reader to stop, and the comma indicates a pause, and while this may seem to be a punctuational contradiction, it is not. The semicolon uses a period to stop the reader, and simultaneously uses a comma to alert the reader that what follows is not a new sentence, but rather a continuation or extension of the thought expressed in the words preceding the mark. The signal to stop in the period is modified by the signal to pause in the comma. There is a very logical method to the madness of placing a period and a comma in one mark of punctuation.

There are two important uses of the semicolon. The first use is to combine two independent clauses, or said another way, they can punctuate a compound sentence without a conjunction. Often the compound sentence combines two independent clauses with a comma and a conjunction as in the sentence example below:

Grammar study is challenging, but many students can profit from the pursuit.

For most compound sentences the use of the comma and conjunction to combine the independent clauses works well. However, when the second clause bears a special, unique, or dramatic relationship to the first clause, a semicolon can be used alone, without a conjunction. Since such relationships are not common to the clauses in all compound sentences, the semicolon should be used sparingly. It is used properly in the example below:

The witness gave her evidence to the jury; they listened spellbound to the last word.

It bears repeating that when the two clauses in a compound sentence share a special bond or link, use of the semicolon is appropriate. Indiscriminately using the semicolon as a joiner of independent clauses weakens writing vitality.

The second use of the semicolon is to separate groups of words that contain items that are themselves separated by commas. This sounds more complicated than it appears, and when you review the example below you will understand how this use of the semicolon is just another aid to compositional clarity. Here is the example:

> Mary test drove the Mustang, a fine sports car; the Dodge Charger, a vintage muscle car; and the Chevrolet Camaro, a legendary tire-burning hot rod.

Semicolons do serve other purposes, but the purposes outlined here are the ones most common and will equip the student writer quite nicely.

8.2.7 Quotation Marks ("and")

As made visible above in the heading of this section, and in the later portions of this sentence, there are "open" quotation marks and "closed" quotation marks. Both exist because quotation marks are always used in pairs. They are always used in pairs because they signal the beginning word or group of words of special interest to the reader, and eventually they signal the ending of that special interest.

There are two common uses of quotation marks. The first is to mark or set-off "direct address," which is the writing-out of the exact words spoken or written by a person other than the actual writer. If the actual writer is a conversant in a dialogue, such as in an interview, than the actual writer's words might also appear in quotation marks. A very simple example of the use of quotation marks in direct address is provided below:

John stood up from his desk and declared, "It's time for lunch!"

John's exact words are enclosed in a pair of quotation marks – opening marks to begin the quotation and closing marks to end it. One annoying variation of this use of quotation marks occurs when a direct address quotation contains another direct address quotation inside of it. When this happens, a set of single (not the standard double) quotation marks is used to mark or set-off the quotation within the quotation. See the examples below:

Mary turned to Susan and shouted, "Mother said, 'Susan has to wash those dishes,' so you had better listen to your mother!"

Professor Smith raised his eyebrows angrily and explained, " It was Hamlet who said, 'To be or not to be...,' not Polonius."

The second most common use of quotation marks is to mark or set off certain words or phrases that are used to express meanings other than their literal meanings. In this use, a reader is warned of the non-standard use of words or phrases by the appearance of the quotation marks. A few examples are shown below:

The "generous reward" ended up being a handshake and a mumbled thank you.

The classical jazz was played very "hot," by musicians who were very "cool."

To win the chess tournament Alexei had to play "down and dirty."

8.2.8 Dash (–)

The dash is a short horizontal line inserted between spaces that usually marks an abrupt shift in the standard tone or flow of the words in a sentence. Dashes are considered by many writers to be too non-traditional for use in formal writing. Nevertheless, they do provide a signal to readers that something unusual is about to be presented. It may be something related to the main idea of the sentence, but it will be a break from the norm. The word "abrupt" is as good a word as there is to describe the writing change incumbent upon the use of a dash. Usually dashes are used in pairs. They begin and then end the abrupt shift from the main idea of a sentence. A large number of examples might help to illustrate the proper use of the dash, but as always, we will "boil down" our examples to a precious few. They are:

If he doesn't win the prize – and he certainly will not – his father will be humiliated.

It was Jefferson – or was it Madison – who contributed to the *Federalist*.

If you enjoy travelling – and who doesn't – take the train to the plane.

8.2.9 Ellipses (...)

Ellipses are three consecutive periods usually used to denote that a certain word or group of words originally included in a line of writing have been removed. They can also be used to show that certain preceding words or concluding words have been left off. See below:

> The Pledge states that we are "...one nation under God...."

Ellipses can show a break from, and then a resumption of, the words in a piece of writing. When in the middle of a sentence, three periods form the ellipses; when an ellipses ends a sentence, a fourth period is added to show the end punctuation.

Another use of ellipses is to express an exaggerated pause for the purpose of showing extended thought or consideration. An example follows:

> Simone should have refused immediately, but she did not want to cause...trouble.

As with several of the other specialized punctuation marks, ellipses should be left in the quiver of punctuation arrows until they can be carefully aimed, launched, and squarely hit their mark.

8.2.10 Apostrophe (')

Apostrophes are used in three grammatical circumstances: (1) to show the possessive form of nouns, (2) to show that certain letters of words have been removed to form contracted words or contractions, and finally, (3) to create certain plural forms of non-words. These three circumstances will be reviewed below.

8.2.10.1 Apostrophes to show possession

As we know, nouns can be either singular or plural in number. Nouns in the plural form usually end with a formulation that includes the letter "s." Apostrophes are used to show the possessive form of nouns both singular and plural. As luck would have it, these possessive forms of nouns end in some formulation that includes an apostrophe and also the letter "s." The confusions accompanying the singular, plural, and possessive forms of nouns, combine to form the most misspelled, mistake-ridden, error-crammed, and utterly muddled aspect of English grammar. Shakespeare himself could hardly have expressed the continuing confusion attendant upon this particular punctuation problem. However, a careful reading of this section will lift readers out this swamp of grammatical ignorance, and elevate them to a knowledge generally unpossessed by our species.

The term "possession" for purposes of grammar, refers to who or what owns, possesses, or controls something capable of being possessed. Harry's gloves belong to or are possessed by Harry. It is the same for the following:

the *book's* cover...
the corporation's employees...
the *weather's* unpredictability...
Sally's shoes...

The above examples contain the possessive forms of the singular nouns which appear in italics. The possessive forms of plural nouns are a bit more confusing because the apostrophe usually moves to the right of the letter "s' that often forms the plural. Plural possessives are more complex, but still understandable. See below:

The four *books'* covers were torn.
The African *lions'* dens are well hidden.
All the *pencils'* points had been broken.

When a noun ends with the letter "s" (as in the proper noun John Evans) the possessive form usually takes an apostrophe only, as in the example, "John Evans' examination paper."

Confusion creeps in when writers become uncertain about whether any particular noun (singular or plural) should or should not be in the possessive form. If it should be possessive, does it need an apostrophe? If it needs one, exactly where does that pesky apostrophe go? A simple (but by no means exhaustive) set of rules for possessive formation follows:

1. Carefully consider whether your noun calls for the possessive (not to be confused with the plural) form.

2. Forming the possessive of any noun requires use of an apostrophe.

3. To form the possessive of singular nouns add an apostrophe and the letter "s."

4. To form the possessive of plural nouns ending in "s" add an apostrophe after the final "s."

5. Proofread carefully and respond appropriately to glaring aberrations.

8.2.10.2 Apostrophes to show removal of letters

Apostrophes are used to write contracted words, also known as contractions. These are words that have been shortened so they can be spoken quickly. For example, the words "do not" become "don't," "cannot" becomes "can't," and "will not," become "won't." The apostrophe replaces certain letters that have been removed to shorten the length and the sound of the original words.

As a general rule, do not use contractions in your formal writing. They are acceptable when writing dialogue, or affecting a conversational style in writing, but should not be used in formal written expressions such as reports, papers and examinations.

8.2.10.3 Apostrophes to form plural of non-words

Apostrophes are also used when creating the plural form of letters, numbers, and other representational figures such as ampersands. The following examples will demonstrate this particular use:

There are five s's in the word possesses.

He believed the numbers on his paycheck deserved to have two more o's added.

8.2.11 The Hyphen (-)

As we know from our previous study, an adjective is a word that adds information to or otherwise modifies a noun. Among its other uses, the hyphen is used to connect two words that appear as a single adjective in front of a noun. These two-word adjectives (an example of which is at the beginning of this very sentence – yes, the word "adjectives" is a plural noun) can be effective tools when a writer finds he or she is searching for a unique description. Compound nouns are also words that employ hyphens. The student-athlete, the philosopher-king, or the child-star are examples of this use of the hyphen.

Other uses of the hyphen include the graphic representation of the spelling of a word, as in the example, i-m-m-i-n-e-n-t. Also, double digit numbers are often represented with the use of a hyphen as in the examples thirty-six and sixty-four.

***

Chapter Eight Nutshell

Punctuation marks are as important to writers and readers as road signs are to travelers. Writers who do not attend to punctuation allow readers to stray from the intended path. They are only little spots of ink or darkness, but used properly, punctuation is the single most clarifying grammatical force.

Chapter Eight Exercise

Visit your local library or go online to your favorite search engine and access a copy of the novel *Tale of Two Cities* by Charles Dickens. The story is set in 18th century England. Carefully read the first paragraph of Chapter Three entitled "The Night Shadows." Read only the first paragraph. One of the major characters of the novel is entering a city at night by stagecoach, and shares his musing thoughts with the reader. Compose an essay not exceeding 100 words that discusses the rambling thoughts of the coach passenger. Do not use direct quotation or paraphrase from any source.

CHAPTER NINE

PARAGRAPHING

9.1 Paragraph Purposes

Paragraphs are to the written page what punctuation marks are to the sentence. They are intentionally and distinctly visible signals to a reader to pay special attention because one main idea has ended and another is about to be introduced. Paragraphs and punctuation marks are signposts set in place by conscientious writers for the benefit of discriminating readers. In the case of the paragraph, the visible signal usually comes in the form of an "indented line." In Standard Written English, this means an opening or first line of writing that begins an inch or so further to the right than subsequent lines. When a reader sees this "indent" he or she will know that a new paragraph has begun.

There are two important inquiries regarding paragraph formation: when should one paragraph leave off, and a new one begin, and what should a completed paragraph contain? If student writers continue to ask these questions throughout composition, the quality and clarity of their writing will be well served. This chapter will treat each of the questions in characteristically fundamental, rather than excruciating, detail.

A paragraph leaves off when a writer believes that the main idea that the paragraph supports has been fully or sufficiently developed. Just as a sentence contains one complete thought, a paragraph contains one main idea. This main idea is usually expressed by a succession of sentences presented in a logical or developmental sequence. If I am doing my job well, the paragraphs in this chapter section are examples of sequentially expressed main ideas. For that matter, every paragraph in every chapter of this book should represent a reasonably good example of a well-developed paragraph. When the writer believes that the main idea has been communicated clearly, the paragraph ends, and the next main idea will be addressed in a new paragraph. If the readers here think that that time has come in this paragraph, they are quite correct.

Poor paragraphing takes two forms; it is poor when a new paragraph is called for, but the writer disregards the call and improperly connects two or more main ideas that should be segregated from one another; paragraphing is equally poor when a writer skips willy-nilly from one paragraph to another before any one particular main idea has run its due course. In both cases poor paragraphing is a serious clarity-kill for a reader. Student writers will often complain that good writing demands so intense a level of concentration, that paragraphing is an afterthought, if it is a thought at all. The result is page upon page of one endless running paragraph that inevitably and completely confuses the reader. If student writing is essentially well composed, but good paragraphing has been neglected, the writer has invested serious capital, only to receive a very poor return on their money.

How does the student writer know whether they have committed paragraphical neglect? Unfortunately there is no rule for determining the proper length of a paragraph. The determination of proper length lies entirely within the discretion of the writer, but good sense and reasonableness should prevail. Although it is not common, a paragraph can be as short as a single sentence. When should a paragraph be that short? The answer is whenever it contains a main idea that clearly needs to stand alone. The answer to the question, "how is the student writer supposed to know if he or she has committed paragraphing error," is axiomatic. They will know by carefully proofreading what they have written. Early on in the text it was noted that writing is labor. There are no short-cuts when it comes to producing quality work in any realm, least of all in the laborious work of letters.

9.2 The Rule of Rules

In the paragraphs above, the need for and importance of paragraphing have been set out, along with the physical element of indention as the demarcation of the paragraph. It is now important to consider the internal structure of the paragraph. As with all matters of writing style – constructing phrases, clauses, selecting modifiers, and combining all these to craft successful sentences – the paragraph works best when it is well organized.

What exactly does the term "well organized" mean? Does it mean "following the rules?" The answer is yes and no. Yes, following the rules usually meets with a good result. However, rules need to be seen for what they are. They are invariably the end product of a long line of trials and errors, and then more trials and more errors. Writing rules do not produce clarity. They are merely the accumulations of ideas that over many years have been shown to affect a clear writing result. Rules are organic things, not artificial things. Writing rules – all language rules – come into existence only after we have discovered what clearly works well. Only after that discovery is made and proven does a rule emerge. Therefore, the "rule of rules" is that rules serve us, they do not bind us. They are what we have collectively decided they should be. Therefore, the only absolute and immutable law of writing is clarity, without which the writer is wasting his or her time and the reader's.

A short continuation of this discussion on writing rules may be helpful at this point. If we can take a short detour from the discussion on paragraphing, let us consider for a moment, one particular rule.

There is a very important rule that states it is best to write sentences in the "active voice." The active voice is the style of sentence construction that places the subject in front of the verb. An example of an active voice sentence is written below:

Alicia questioned the candidate.

The active voice rule states that the example above is the proper way to write a sentence, and is superior to using the "passive voice." An example of the same sentence written in the passive voice is below:

The candidate was questioned by Alicia.

The "rule" that states "active voice" sentences are best was not arbitrarily fabricated by some enlightened rule-maker. It grew out long experience with our English language and our linguistic culture. At this point in our language history it is reasonably understood that our minds are better at processing groups of words that contain a subject first, followed by a verb-predicate. The rule follows what works best. Active voice sentences are direct; passive voice sentences are more "round about." The rule is a good one, but like all language rules, the active voice rule has grown organically from the long trial and error of what best serves reader clarity.

Kindly excuse this brief "rule" detour. It has now come to an end and we will resume our presentation of paragraphing...rules.

9.3 Paragraph Structure

There are a few simple rules that will assist the student writer in building strong, self-sustaining paragraphs. The basic structure of a beginning, a middle, and an end, is one in which the human mind has always taken comfort. This three-tier developmental form has perfect application to the paragraph. If a paragraph will contain multiple sentences – as most do – the three part structure is best. It includes an opening (beginning) sentence, developing (middle) sentences, and a closing (end) sentence.

9.3.1 The Opening Sentence Introduces the Paragraph

An opening sentence or topic sentence or thesis sentence (the term is immaterial) introduces the intention of the paragraph. Not unlike the active voice sentence, the three part paragraph places the important element first. Unless there is good cause to do so, do not keep readers in suspense. Give them an opening sentence that reveals the essence of the paragraph's main idea. The opening sentence need not detail all the elements of the main idea, but it should offer a glimpse or a hint of them.

9.3.2 Middle Sentences Develop the Paragraph

Once the opening sentence draws aside the curtain, a set of developing sentences should put some color and texture to the landscape of the main idea. If the propriety of a particular order or system of presentation occurs to the writer (eg. an historical or chronological order, a narrative approach, a step-by-step exposition, etc.), that order or system should be employed. These sentences should not be written in ways that isolate them from each other. Rather, they should "transition" smoothly, one sentence to the next. This can be accomplished by the careful use of selective conjunctive adverbs and transitional phrases. A selected list of these are provided below:

SOME CONJUNCTIVE ADVERBS	SOME TRANSITIONAL PHRASES
therefore	on the other hand
nevertheless	for example
however	in other words
consequently	at the same time
besides	in fact

9.3.3 The Closing Sentence Concludes the Paragraph

When presentation of the main idea through the middle sentences is complete, a concluding sentence may be used to make that completion clear. A concluding sentence may be used to draw attention to a particular result or consequence of the middle sentences, point to a reasonable deduction or speculation, or state a warning, inference, or theory suggested by the main idea developed in the middle sentences. The concluding sentence may also be used as a transition to the main idea of the next paragraph. Using the concluding sentence as a transition to the next main idea is especially helpful when the main ideas in successive paragraphs are connected to an expansive general theme. In any event, a concluding sentence should alert the reader that the main idea of the paragraph is drawing to a close and a "new" main idea is close at hand.

The reader may have noticed that the exercises in this volume are based almost exclusively on selected paragraphs of writing from some of the world's great authors. The selections are short in length, but they are characteristically great. The greatness of a writer is as visible in one of their paragraphs as in an entire shelf of their volumes. Paragraphs are telling. They are the framed showcases of well written sentences. Writing your sentences with care is not enough; assembling them into the sturdy frame of a paragraph completes the picture.

***

Chapter Nine Nutshell

Paragraphing is to the page what punctuation is to the sentence. Paragraphs are road signs and guide posts to the changes in a writer's thoughts. The clear development of the main ideas of a writing depend entirely upon paragraphing. Pages full of well written sentences will not cure the defects of poor paragraphing. All the parts of the language arts machine need to be in their proper places.

Chapter Nine Exercise

Visit your local library or go online to your favorite search engine and access the 1931 U.S. Supreme Court case entitled <u>McBoyle v. US</u> written by Chief Justice Holmes (283 US 25). The case concerns review of Mr. McBoyle's conviction for transporting a stolen airplane from one state to another. Justice Holmes reverses the conviction and sets Mr. McBoyle free. Carefully read the entire two page court decision. Compose an essay not exceeding 100 words that explains why Justice Holmes reversed the lower court conviction and found defendant McBoyle not guilty. Do not use direct quotation or paraphrase from any source.

STYLE ELEMENTS TO EMBRACE

Introduction

"Style" is a difficult word to define because it refers to the unique qualities that people attach to common or ordinary accomplishment. Many of us sing or dance. Others may play an instrument. Still others can paint, design, write, plan a garden, or build a chair. Each of these activities calls for performing many repetitively common actions, yet we all perform these common actions in hosts of uncommon and distinctly individual ways. When those uncommon ways of performing a common act combine to create a strikingly recognizable individuality, that individuality is called style. We may say of a painter that he or she has a "unique style." A building, or a piece of music, or a novel, a garden, or a chair may have an "unmistakable style." "Unique" and "unmistakable" are interesting adjectives, but they do not much clarify the difficult matter of understanding our noun. When we say a style is "unmistakable" or "unique," we may mean that it is easily recognized, but being able to quickly recognize something is not the same as knowing what it is.

In writing, style is a term no less intellectually elusive than in any other creative-based human activity. However, if we can agree that style is something visible and tangible, we can at least discuss those visible tangible aspects of style in writing.

There are two parts to writing style. There is the style that is achieved by the way a writer uses mechanical or grammatical conventions, and then there is the less visible, less tangible style a writer achieves by sheer art. For what it is worth, we will take a stab at discussing the artistic aspects of writing style in the next chapter (Chapter 11). Thankfully, this chapter plants its feet firmly on the more solid ground of mechanical, grammatical style.

10.1 Revisit Chapters 1 Through 9

The preceding chapters of this book contain many of the foundations of English language grammar. Believe it or not, developing a distinctive writing style begins with understanding parts of speech because (if you will excuse the cliché) they are the building blocks of language. Each of the other eight chapters following the first is designed to offer some familiarity with the technical knowledge the student writer will need to write well. There is simply no substitute for knowledge of base-line rules – not for gardeners, carpenters, lighting designers, musicians, painters, electricians, athletes, and least of all, writers.

In your present circumstances, you may be correct in proclaiming yourself a competent (even proficient) college level writer. If you are, move forward with confidence. If you are not, you may want to revisit the earlier chapters of this book. Review them with conviction. If the fundamental treatment in this text is in any way insufficient, seek out a more detailed, a more comprehensive text, and graciously take what it has to offer. Writing, in some form and to at least some degree, will be the eventual work product of every college educated person. Employers expect a college graduate to be capable of higher level thinking and higher level communication. Prepare yourself to meet and exceed that expectation. It may come in the form of a simple report, a newsletter item, a message to staff, an explication of policy, a routine evaluation, or a simple business letter, but it will come. Write it well, and with recognizable style, and promotion and occupational advance will follow as surely as sweet follows sugar.

10.2 Outlining

Before style can be achieved, clarity must prevail, and nothing serves clarity better than good structure and sound organization. Structure and organization are themselves two of the most complimentary elements of style. A writer who can clearly explain a complex policy statement, or compress intricate, detailed data into accessible, unambiguous language, has a skill that is worth its weight in precious metals. Next in importance to knowing the rules of the writing road as presented in our first nine chapters, is the ability to organize. A simple pre-writing outline is the first step in any sizable writing assignment, academic or otherwise. The specific outline form a writer may use is a matter of personal choice, but some initial organizational model must be employed. A check list is provided below for purpose of example. The items noted here may or may not be applicable depending upon the vagaries of the assignment, but the general concepts are of indubitable value. In each and every sizable writing assignment the writer should:

1. Secure a comprehensive understanding of all aspects of the physical writing task including: assignment length, assignment purpose, submission deadlines, identity of the end-reader, evaluator, or audience, necessary level of formality, appropriate tone, need for academic formatting, potential publishing concerns, etc.;
2. Contact the assigning authority (professor, supervisor, etc.) to confirm the writer's understanding of each of the above aspects of the assignment, and the dates for completion of the

anticipated tasks that will meet or precede the actual submission deadlines;

3. Construct a list of time-line priorities. Outline the project in stages that include: a general statement of the topic treated, a formulation of a thesis in regard to the topic, lists of items that stand in defense of (and perhaps in opposition to) the thesis, and a prioritized listing of the items generated in the lists above;

4. Gather all necessary collateral data pertaining to the thesis, including research as necessary, while checking deadlines;

5. Write the body of the assignment, while keeping an eye on the deadline clock; and

6. Proofread, correct, modify, and re-write while checking deadlines.

A well-developed outline is a reliable and consistent time-saving device. A relatively small investment of time at the front- end of the project will avoid endless irritating delays and consequential problems thereafter. The outline is the signpost that we must vigilantly keep within our sight. It should remain in full view and keep us securely on the right path throughout our compositional journey. Follow the outline scrupulously, and as you write, follow all the rules for grammar and style set forth in all the above chapters. Structure and organization are a writer's best friends.

10.3 Parallel Structure

The basis of the rule for parallel structure is simple enough to understand, but difficult to apply when we are in a fever to get our words onto paper or screen before they fly out of our minds. When the fever rises, we tend to scribble out our words in a flurry. We quickly forget many of the important rules, and then we conveniently forget that we have forgotten them. The result is groupings of words that stumble and trip over each other, much to the irritation, dismay, and confusion of our readers.

The rule of parallel structure states that words or groups of words within a sentence that are similar in form or serve a similar function should be presented in the same grammatical format. The example immediately below illustrates a violation of the rule:

NON PARALLEL STRUCTURE
Sam likes swimming, cycling, and to play tennis. (bad)

-also-

Sam likes to swim, cycling, and playing tennis. (bad)

Sam likes three forms of exercise. All three forms should be presented in the same grammatical format. In the examples above they are not, and so the sentence violates the parallel structure rule. Two of the exercises (swimming and cycling) are in the form of gerunds ("ing" nouns), and the last exercise is stated in the form of an infinitive. The parallel structure rule tells us that when multiple words or phrases are parts of a sentence, gerunds should be kept with gerunds, infinitives with infinitives, nouns with nouns, verbs with verbs, and so on. The correct forms of the sentence are shown below:

PARALELL STRUCTURE
Sam likes swimming, cycling, and playing tennis. (good)

-also-

Sam likes to swim, to cycle, and to play tennis. (good)

When it comes down to it, multiple similar grammatical terms in a sentence prefer their own company. Keep like forms together. If a sentence with a listing of multiple terms sounds choppy or somehow disconnected, the chances are good that there is a violation of parallel structure. Checking the parallel structure of multiple terms in a sentence is one of many sure-fire ways to maintain a clear writing style.

10.4 Vocabluary

"Vocabulary" refers to the depth of the pool from which a writer draws his or her words. The words writers choose contribute significantly to the focus, tone, shape, and texture of their writing. A writer's word choices may seem spontaneous, but often they are the result of very careful consideration. In this respect, a writer's choice of words is a direct function of the writer's personal style. If student writers have an extensive vocabulary, they can select just the right words to expresses their ideas. A good vocabulary allows a writer to distinguish between very delicate shades of meaning, or make subtle or very precise points in an argument. A limited vocabulary reduces word choices, and the potential for precision is correspondingly restricted. Possessing a broad vocabulary does not insure good writing, nor does it improve a writer's style. Many great books were written with simple uncomplicated words and sentences. Nevertheless, it remains true that the more words we have at our command, the better equipped we are to write well. Vocabulary is therefore one of several functions of good writing style.

If I were pressed to characterize the vocabulary of my personal writing style, the adjective I would use to describe it would be "pedantic." For those of you who are unfamiliar with it, the word "pedantic" is not very flattering. It means "stuffy" and somewhat "arrogant." It comes from the root word "pedant." A pedant is a teacher who occasionally thinks too highly of himself, a description that in my own case is not altogether misplaced. My writing style is pedantic because I regularly violate one of the cardinal rules of style in regard to vocabulary. That rule states, "Do not use a fancy word when a simple word will serve as well." When given the choice between choosing a simple word or a fancy word, I usually choose the fancy word. It is my belief that when communicating language to students, a teacher has an obligation to instruct, and good instruction should encourage student learning. If teachers used only simple words, students would have less cause to discover the wonderfully deep word pool of the English language.

More words mean more choices, and more choices improve our chances to make the kinds of fine distinctions that some ideas demand. Therefore, improve your writing style potential by acquiring an enlarged vocabulary. This can be accomplished by memorizing lists of words along with their definitions (boring), or by committing yourself to a steady diet of high quality reading (exciting).

10.5 Figures of Speech

Figures of speech are not parts of speech. An unsuspecting student might confuse them, but they are as different as bees are from bottles. As we know from our study of Chapter Two, parts of speech are words that we have created to express the functions of words in sentences. Their essential nature is technical, grammatical, and functional. Completely on the other hand, figures of speech are amusing little writing devices designed to enhance, embellish, or otherwise decorate our written expressions. Their essential nature is purely imaginative, artistic, and creative.

There are many figures of speech. With the exception of the writing done in creative writing classes, most student writing will contain few if any figures of speech. For our purposes (which continue to be presentation of what is "fundamental"), this section will review only three of the more common figures of speech.

A metaphor is a direct comparison of two ordinarily dissimilar things for the purpose of presenting a startling or unique idea or image. The dissimilar elements are underlined in the examples below:

METAPHOR

His <u>voice</u> was a <u>trumpet</u> sounding down the valley.

Lucille's violin is the bedrock upon which the orchestra was built.

A simile is a comparison of two ordinarily dissimilar things for the purpose of presenting a startling or unique idea or image that includes the words "like" or "as." The dissimilar elements are in italics in the examples below:

SIMILE

For Sophie, the *one-room apartment* was as beautiful as the *Taj Mahal.*

His *meager wages* were like *a king's treasure*
in the pocket of his jeans.

A hyperbole is a statement containing a gross exaggeration or overstatement. The exaggeration in the examples below should be obvious:

HYPERBOLE

His arms stuck a mile out of his sleeves.

I am so hungry I could eat a horse.

Figures of speech are designed for creative or artistic effect. Aside from the occasional creative writing class, they do not often serve the staid purposes of formal, business, or professional writing. Student writers should use figures of speech sparingly, if they use them at all. Occasionally, a relevant and appropriately inserted figure of speech can be an important style element of student writing. However, student writers should almost always avoid the impulse to write in a dramatic, humorous, witty, or entertaining style. Those styles of writing depend heavily upon liberal use of the figures of speech. A formal, academic style is far more suitable for most assigned student writing. Therefore, do your student writing style a favor and exercise discretion in your use of figures of speech.

***

Chapter Ten Nutshell

It has been said - and it was well said - that there is no such thing as good writing, only good editing. The sections of Chapter 10 are testaments to the wisdom of this epigram. All writing is an indelible imprint and reflection of its author. Adopt the habit of re-reading and revising, and you will always be putting your best writing foot forward.

Chapter Ten Exercise

Visit your local library or go online to your favorite search engine and access a good translation of the *Dialogues of Plato*. Turn to the dialogue entitled *Crito*. This short exchange is between a student (Crito) and his teacher (Socrates). Socrates is in prison and is determined to drink poison and accept his prescribed death sentence. Crito tries desperately to dissuade him. Carefully read through their discussion and decide for yourself whose argument is the stronger, Crito's or Socrates'. Compose an essay not exceeding 100 words that explains why you believe that either Crito or Socrates is correct. Do not use direct quotation or paraphrase from any source.

STYLE ELEMENTS TO AVOID

11.1 **Wordiness**

One of the most prominent negative characteristics of college student writing is wordiness. It is a problem most apparent when a student has been asked to complete a lengthy assignment. In some small part, college writing instructors are to blame because they invariably assign large writing projects. This in turn causes students to become riddled with fear and anxiety. The inevitable result is a student submission short on substance and long on words. Strangely enough, students seem to believe that their blatant demonstrations of wordiness are perfectly concealed from their reader. The simple fact is that expressing few ideas in many words is as visible to most readers as the color green.

One common example of wordiness is the "filler phrase." This is a group of words that adds lots of extra letters but no extra thoughts to a sentence. Some examples of filler phrases are below (the unnecessary words are in italics):

> *While it may be very difficult for anyone to honestly believe it was at all possible,* John failed.

> *There can be very little doubt in the minds of every person who has ever thought about it, that* taxation is onerous.

> *Anyone who has ever seriously considered the circumstances of the situation will immediately concede, that* war is hell.

Student writers should express ideas without the use of filler phrases. Simplicity is best, clarity must prevail, and obfuscation should suffer a swift and painful death.

11.2 Redundancy and Excessive Explanation

Once an idea has been presented clearly, a writer should move on. Teachers are often the greatest offenders of the rule against redundancy. They feel it is their duty to repeat (and repeat, and repeat) the important parts of lessons so that students will be sure to get the message. Despite the best of intentions, redundancy in writing should be avoided. Yes, some complex ideas require special attention and may be misunderstood by the reader unless several explanations are provided from various perspectives. Such delineation is not considered redundancy. However, reasonably simple concepts can be and should be made clear in short order. Examples of redundancy follow:

Speak clearly so you can be understood and not confuse anyone. (bad)

Speak clearly. (good)

Excessive explanation is a form of redundancy and should be avoided. The student writer needs to acquire confidence in their ability to express ideas clearly. Over-explaining an idea, or re-clarifying a point after it has been made, shows the lack of confidence in a writer, and irritates a reader.

11.3 Over-Reliance on Modifiers

A good writer spends more time selecting appropriate nouns and verbs than selecting modifiers to shape and color them. The best adjective in the world cannot redeem a poorly chosen noun, and wonderful adverbs do not fortify a weak verb. Writers are well advised to put their best efforts into selecting effective nouns and precise verbs, and leave modifiers as icing on the cake. Strings of modifiers are annoying things.

11.4 Slang, Jargon, Cliché

Slang

Slang describes words ordinarily reserved for spoken language. Slang is informal at best, and common, coarse, and occasionally profane at worst. It is wonderful when used to colorfully decorate our speech, and it may be very effectively used in the dialogue of creative writing, but slang is anathema to most formal student writing. Slang words come into and go out of the spoken vocabulary so quickly that a listing of them here would soon be stale and out of date. Any word that has a decidedly conversational tone to it should be avoided when writing a formal student paper. True that!

Jargon

Jargon is a body of specialized vocabulary that has been embraced by a particular field of study and may often include ordinary words that have been assigned a special meaning in that field. When a student is writing in such a field, the use of jargon is perfectly acceptable. However, when writing a general interest paper the use of jargon is considered academically disingenuous and intellectually pretentious. It is in compositional bad taste to subject unsuspecting readers to a vocabulary they can hardly be expected to appreciate or understand. As with slang, jargon in its proper place serves an important purpose. Out of that place, it is a discourtesy to the reader.

Cliché

A cliché is a witty expression, the overuse of which has rendered it virtually worthless. When we hear or read a cliché we usually roll our eyes and click our tongues in disgust. When the words that form the cliché were first uttered or first written, they were truly quality expressions, but that quality was their downfall. People became enamored of them, used them endlessly year after year, and a cliché was born. Good writing avoids the use of the cliché.

11.5 Sexist Language

Examples of sexist language occur when a word representing one sex is used to represent both sexes, as in the sentence example below:

> A writer needs to be conscientious if he hopes to be successful.

The masculine pronoun "he" in a sentence where the subject is neither masculine nor feminine, is presumptuous. It presumes that women are not writers. Sexist language should be avoided, although precisely how to avoid it has not been conclusively decided. One obstacle is formulating a word that can resolve the problem in the sentence example noted above. If the subject of a sentence is singular as "A writer" is, what singular pronoun can be used? The use of "he" is decidedly sexist language; the use of "she" is also sexist language, although there is support for the claim that the historical overuse of the masculine pronoun might be reasonably corrected by corresponding overuse of the feminine pronoun. Writers often choose to avoid the conflict in one of two ways: either they regularly use plural subjects and then supply the non-sexist pronouns such as "they," "them," and "their," or they apply both singular pronoun forms to the singular subject, namely "he and/or she," or "she and/or he." Attempts to invent and introduce new non-sexist singular pronouns such as "s/he," "hir" and "shhe," have met with only limited success. Sexist language is a problem waiting for a conclusive solution.

11.6 Unconventional Argument

Student writers are often anxious to display their purported intellectual prowess. This is a natural inclination and should be indulged whenever possible. However, in the interests of earning good grades and preserving their blossoming intellectual reputations, students should season their impulse to impress readers with reasonableness and rationality. Unconventional argument may be an interesting stretch for the student mind, but it should not snap the rubber band of reason. In order to secure and hold a reader's interest, writers need to maintain argumentative credibility. Presentation of an unconventional argument can be a fascinating addition to a formal written document, but it should be an addition to, not the exclusive element of, a well written paper.

11.7 Opinionated Expression

Unless you have been invited or assigned to compose a writing that is in the nature of an "Op-Ed" (Opinion-Editorial) column, or you are writing a book of your own design, you should not presume to inject your writing with personal opinion. In most writing formulations the overt expression of personal opinion tries the patience of the reader. Even if you are fortunate enough to have your material in the hands of a sympathetic reader, unsolicited personal opinion is almost always tedious and overbearing. In the ordinary course of exposing your personal writing style, your personal opinions will subtly and inevitably winnow their way into your reader's consciousness. Allowing for that subtly is enough. Brash declarations of personal opinion will be resisted by most reasonably minded readers.

11.8 Stereotyping

Stereotyping is assigning the characteristics of an individual to an entire classification or group of persons. Even if the characteristics assigned are not particularly negative or discrediting, the presumption that they apply to all members of the subject group is prejudicial. A sentence example of negative stereotyping follows:

Those Italian immigrants certainly love their garlic and olive oil.

In most of its various forms, stereotyping is a sure way to damage or destroy a writer's credibility with the general reading public. However, stereotyping can be occasionally tolerated or even admired. An example of its tolerance and admiration is to write material that characterizes firefighters as courageous, soldiers as brave, doctors as compassionate, or teachers as....smart. If the characteristics are negative, or if they intentionally isolate or segregate the referenced group, stereotyping becomes inimical.

11.9 Style Imitation

All of us have been exposed to the styles of many gifted writers, from the ancient to the modern, the philosophic to the comedic, and the poetic to the scientific. The styles of these writers have made their impressions on us is ways we may or may not be willing to admit. In any event, out personal writing style is bound to be influenced by the styles of others that we admire. If I could write poetry, I would want to write it as it was written by John Donne. It matters little to me that Donne lived and wrote 400 years ago; my poetry would look and sound as much like his as I could make it. In writing, admiration for a writer's style is one thing; imitation is altogether another. Writers must write in ways natural to their mind's disposition. Imitation may be the highest form of flattery, but then flatters are the people we should trust least and avoid most.

11.10 Self Aggrandizement

This section of chapter 11 is one with which I struggle. The preceding sentence is a perfect example of my struggle, as I have used the personal pronoun "I." The general rule for good writing is for writers to keep themselves in the background. Personal pronouns such as "I," and "me," are frowned upon because they encourage the reader to acknowledge the person of the writer, and this in turn distracts from the idea of the writing. The rule is sound. In the case of formal writing, especially student academic writing, a disembodied writer is a good writer. The famous 17th

Century French essayist Michael du Montaigne would heartily disagree, but one exception in 400 years is no basis upon which to violate an otherwise valid rule. Write disembodied.

11.11 Mystery Tour

Avoid as much as possible the occasional temptation to keep your reader in the dark. Writers are often jealous of the information they possess and they decide to whet a reader's appetite by waiting to the last possible moment to reveal some important piece of the writing puzzle. Unless you are an accomplished writer of mystery stories (and few students are), unreasonably withholding information from your reader is detrimental to reader and writer alike. Structuring the revelation of certain material can be an essential element of writing clarity. However, do not allow your writing to become a mystery tour of unanswered questions and cryptic predictions. Do not disguise your ideas. Tell your reader what you are thinking. Once again, these are not recommendations for a novelist or journalist. They are simple plans that will assist the student writer in composing clear straightforward academic prose.

***

Chapter Eleven Nutshell

Bad habits are hard to break and so avoiding the temptation to form them in the first place is easiest and best. A character in a Shakespeare play might refer to the bad habits listed in the sections of this chapter as "portents and evils imminent," and so they are. We should avoid them or indulge them only sparingly in unique writing circumstances. Proofreading is required to root them out, and precious time is needed to right their wrongs.

Chapter Eleven Exercise

Visit your local library or go online to your favorite search engine and access a copy of the poems of Walt Whitman. Turn to the poem entitled *When I Heard the Learn'd Astronomer*. The poet apparently attended an astronomy lecture that left quite an impression on him. Read the poem slowly and carefully several times, paying special attention to the signals provided by punctuation. Compose an essay not exceeding 100 words that describes what general impression Whitman was left with after he "...Heard the Learn'd Astonomer." Do not use direct quotation or paraphrase from any source.

ACADEMIC MANUSCRIPT STYLES

12.1 Purposes Served

Academic research and writing are the food, clothing, and shelter of human learning. Without them, the people who do the heavy mental lifting would have no record of what they think. With them, one thinker can read and learn what every other thinker has thought, think through those earlier thoughts, and build up something new. Research and writing aim at revealing truth. There is no higher human pursuit. Many of these attempts fail, some few succeed in part, none have ever fully hit the true mark, but every piece of scholarly writing – including student composed scholarship – presumes to take careful aim at truth. It is important work and needs to be documented carefully so that a reliable, credible record is created and preserved.

The words reliable and credible are interdependent terms and deserve closer examination. Academic writing is reliable when it contains data that is traceable in a clear straight line, back to an utterly *bone fide* source. To begin with, a source is *bone fide* when it is actual and genuine – when it exists in space and time and is what it purports to be. Also, a *bone fide* source is one that was developed in reliance upon previous sources that were themselves *bone fide*, and so on. This continuing chain of *bone fide* sources builds the reliability that is an absolute requisite of research writing. When reliability is established as manifested in the detailed record provided by manuscript formatting, the work becomes more and more believable, or credible. The reliability created by a strict adherence to academic manuscript style, helps to establish credibility. Credibility does not necessarily mean that the thesis and conclusions of the writing are to be believed, but that the foundations of the work supporting the conclusions are reasonably worthy of belief.

The student will do little writing work of greater importance than research writing. It is the axle of the wheel that rolls on toward the truth awaiting us in hundreds of research fields (I have just ignored my own advice to use figures of speech sparingly). A student's own contribution to that truth-journey is no small matter.

Formal student research papers or term papers, especially undergraduate papers, are important opportunities for the student to glimpse part of the purpose of the academic world. Research writing calls for application of all the same writing rules and plans set forth in the chapters previous. However, the research writing product is a hybrid because of what it attempts to do, and how it is expected to do it. The fundamental versions of some of those rules follow below.

12.2 A Variety of Styles

There are four (4) major styles of academic manuscript formatting. They are as follows:

1. the Modern Language Association (MLA) style;
2. the American Psychological Association (APA) style;
3. the American Sociological Association (ASA) style; and
4. the Chicago style.

Every field of academic study selects one of these four styles and adopts it as their own. Each style dictates the exact production details to be followed if a writer intends to submit a formal research document in that particular field. These production details include such things as the width of margins, the size and style of font, the accepted way to quote from another author's work, and the form or "style" to use when documenting the information about a relied-upon source.

Strict adherence to the rules of the specific style apply equally to students writing research papers, and to professors writing articles for academic journals. As noted above, these styles exist to insure that the scholarly work done in a particular field is reliable. Reliability and credibility are the cornerstones of research writing and are the primary objectives of each of the academic manuscript styles.

The details inherent in the four styles differ only slightly from one another. Nevertheless, every discipline inflexibly demands that all academic submissions in its field scrupulously adhere to the style it has adopted as its own. The arts and humanities generally embrace either the Modern Language Association (MLA) or Chicago style. Business schools tend to adopt the American Sociological Association (ASA) format style, and the sciences usually select the American Psychological Association (APA) format. It is therefore incumbent upon a student writer to know for certain which style is required for the specific research document they are called upon to write. As a student moves from courses in one field to courses in another, it is almost certain that the manuscript style required will change. Keep in mind that selection of manuscript style is not a matter of student personal choice or familiarity. The selection is made by the cognoscenti in the field and must be accepted stoically by the student writer. A careful reading of the instructions that accompany a course assignment, or a simple inquiry directed to the course instructor is the most reliable way to determine which style is required.

12.3 Common Style Elements

There are five elements standard in most student research documents. They are as follows:

12.3.1. Title page;

12.3.2. Abstract;

12.3.3. Body;

12.3.4. Conclusion; and

12.3.5. Documentation of Sources.

These five elements appear in some form in all MLA, Chicago, APA, and ASA style documents. They may have specialized names or contain subdivisions, but they are common to all styles. Depending upon the length of the document there may be additional elements such as a "Table of Contents," "Glossary," "Table of Figures," "Appendix," and "Bibliography," but the five listed above are accepted research paper staples (that is, "staples" as in "bread and butter," not paper-attachment devices).

The remainder of this chapter will review the five common elements listed above, but the reader is hereby duly cautioned; do not rely upon this outline to present the multitudinous details of a particular manuscript style. What is offered here is a slim overview of common style elements, not a listing of the requirements of any one style. To acquire a thorough understanding of the MLA, Chicago, APA, or ASA style, students must secure a text dedicated to that exact style and study it exclusively.

12.3.1 The Title Page

Every title page for a student submitted research document contains six (6) informational components. The arrangement of the components varies from style to style, but the substance of the information is constant. The six (6) pieces of information are set forth below:

1. the title of the document;
2. the name of the author (the student);
3. the number, section, and full title of the course;
4. the full name of the instructor who assigned the paper;
5. the name of the college or university; and
6. the date the document is due for submission.

These six components should be both centered and balanced on the title page. Centering means that each component should be placed on the page so that the spaces to the right and left of the printed line are equal. Of course the one inch margin rule for the page should never be compromised, but centering all the title page components is essential. Centering has to do with the right-left justification on the title page. An orderly title page will not transform a poor paper into a quality paper, but neither will it distract the reader from appreciating the quality that may be there.

In addition to each line being centered left to right, each one of the six components should be balanced. Balancing is top to bottom justification of the completed page. The title of the paper is at or near the top of the page and five succeeding components are placed below it with spaces between them that are reasonably equal. With proper centering and balancing the title page looks professional and esthetically pleasant. It shows that due care was taken in positioning the information and makes access to the information easy. A sloppy, poorly centered, unbalanced title page sends a disappointing message to the reader. A writer should proudly display his or her attention to detail and organization in the title page.

12.3.2 The Abstract

An abstract is a short writing that briefly explains the purpose of the full length document it precedes. The abstract should not exceed one typewritten page. It does not define terms, state a position, or defend a conclusion. It is simply a short collection of sentences that introduces the main idea of the paper to the reader. It is the paper's main idea in a "nutshell" form. It presents the question the paper will attempt to answer, or the problem it will address, and it does this without prejudice or bias.

The abstract page of a research document should never reveal how a writer feels about the research topic. Feelings are perfectly appropriate for poets, novelists, and journalists, but not for research writers. Research is science, not emotion. Many research topics touch upon themes very affecting to the human heart – themes that quickly and understandably evoke sympathy and pity. The student research writer must put emotionality aside and remain focused on analysis and systematic evaluation. He or she should assume a clinical disposition toward the material. This begins with the words and tone of the abstract.

As with all six (6) components, the Abstract is written with the reader in mind. Readers engaged in doing their own research need to quickly determine whether a particular document is important to their area of study. A well written abstract provides these reading researchers with a one-page overview of what may be a 25 page report. In the few minutes it takes to read an abstract, an astute researcher/reader can decide whether the document is germane to their work.

A carefully composed abstract introduces your writing style, offers a glimpse of the topic and its treatment, and allows researching readers to quickly decide whether or not your research might assist them in their research.

12.3.3 The Body

The major writing element of the student research document is the body of the paper. The body is the showcase of a student's writing style from phrases, clauses, and sentences, to spelling, punctuation, and paragraphs. Of course, as we have repeated endlessly in all the previous chapters, clarity is king. It must be there in the line by line and page by page progression of words. However, when considering the body - the single most important component of the research writing document - the key to overall writing success is good documentary organization.

Paragraphing plays its part in good organization, but in a longer work such as a full bodied research paper, good organization is larger than just good paragraphing. It means arranging arguments, facts, materials, and evidence in ways that build a main idea slowly and surely. Good organization is selecting reliable research to support your paper's position, and then presenting that research in a sequence that persuades your reader toward your conclusions. Good organization may mean providing special headings to tangibly categorize your materials, and perhaps providing subheadings if still further categories are needed. It means presenting the strength of research that supports your conclusions, and perhaps exposing the weakness of research that opposes them.

The body of the paper demands care and time and concentration, and it demands a thorough proofreading. Writing and proofreading and revising an entire research document is not for the faint of heart. Once the student has finished the exhaustive task of writing it, the idea of going back and proofreading the entire text can be daunting. This is when the going gets tough and the tough need to get going (Cliché!). Step away from the keyboard for a day or two or an hour or two, take a few deep breaths, and then proofread, proofread, proofread. It is a chore to be sure, but usually you will find it is not nearly as difficult as writing. Even when proofreading is done with great care, it goes along rather quickly. Refusing to proofread your research paper is not a wise option. Avoid proofreading and revision of the body of your document, and so much of the hard work you have done will be lost to errors that could often have been corrected with the mere push of a button.

12.3.4 The Conclusion

Ordinarily, the conclusion page should be about as long as the abstract; it should not exceed one page. The conclusion page is where we allow logic and reason free reign. If we have presented our arguments and entered our evidence in the body of the paper, the conclusion page will almost write itself. We announced our topic on the title page, introduced the issues of the main idea in the abstract, presented reliable research and supporting facts to aim at truth in the body, and now we offer what truth and learning have led us to believe in the conclusion. It is not a summary of the body, and it is not a restatement of the abstract. The conclusion is sharing with the reader the somewhat hidden message that our research has revealed. It is the culmination of our work and the purpose of it.

12.3.5 Documentation of Sources

Documentation of research sources is challenging to say the least. To begin with, "sources" are the published articles and books that a student writer relies on to write a research paper. These sources are the work of experts in the topic field. They are works that have appeared in book form or as articles in peer-reviewed, academic journals. Generally, when an instructor assigns a formal research or term paper, the sources must be either books, academic journal articles, or a combination of both; newspaper columns, news magazine stories, and materials from informal on-line blogs are ordinarily unacceptable. It is good practice for students to know beforehand precisely what kinds of source materials are appropriate to the project. If in doubt, ask the instructor directly what sources are recommended. Once the student has secured a sufficient number of relevant sources, work on writing the paper can begin in earnest.

Documentation of sources is a two-stage process. Evidence of the first stage can be seen throughout the body or "text" of the paper and is known as "in-text citation." If the student is writing a paragraph of the body and either directly or indirectly uses the information from one of the sources they have gathered, they need to give credit to the author of that source. This credit takes the form of placing the author's last name in reasonably close proximity to the information taken from that author.

The four manuscript styles (MLA, Chicago, APA, and ASA) all have slight variations regarding proper "in-text" citation. All the styles require the credited author's last name. Then each style calls for either a year of publication, the page number from the original text, or some other identifying data. All styles keep the "in-text citation" as short as possible so that the reader of the paper is not too long distracted from the student author's presentation of ideas.

"In-text citation" is a very brief, quick reference that gives credit to the book or article author the student writer has relied upon. This first stage of the documentation process is critical. If it is intentionally excluded, a legal claim of plagiarism can be lodged against the student writer. Research work, even at the student level, is intimately entwined with intellectual property law. This is serious business. Never fail to give credit in the body of your paper to an author upon whose work you have relied.

The second stage of documenting sources works in perfect union with the first stage, and is the natural extension of the first. In the first stage, a relied upon author's last name is provided in the text to give the author due credit. However, the last name alone is hardly enough information for an inquisitive reader. The reader of your paper is entitled to know much more. In addition to knowing the last name of the relied upon author, the reader deserves to know precisely how to access the book or article that is being relied on and referred to. The first stage "in-text" citation cannot provide all that data because the very length of it in the body would seriously interrupt the reader's concentration. Therefore, all four styles agree that readers should be allowed to read through a paper with only the slight interruption of the relied upon author's last name in the "in-text" cite. Then, on the last page of the paper, the last names of all the "in-text" cited authors will be alphabetized and placed on a list along with all the detailed information about the relied upon author that a reader could possibly want. This page is known as the "Works Cited" or "References" (documentation) page. In addition to the relied upon author's full name, the documentation page includes such things as the full title of the author's work, full publication data, volume and page numbers, dates of publication, translator's or editor's names, etc., etc., etc. This is where the full story of the sources is told, a story only hinted at by the abbreviated "in-text citation."

As you may have guessed, the four manuscript styles have annoyingly different ideas about what, how, when, and whether or not information is set forth on the documentation page. However, in the midst of their idiosyncratic variations, there do emerge certain constants.

If the student writer has consulted five sources, there will be five separate entries on the documentation page, one entry for each source. The entries on the documentation page are usually two to four lines of print in length, depending upon (for example) the longness or shortness of the title of the relied upon work. All four styles agree that the entry on the documentation page will be written in three "sentences." These are not sentences in a grammatical sense, but rather "sentences" in the sense that they are groups of information separated by periods. They are sentences only in a "graphic," not in a grammatical, sense of the word.

The three "sentences" of each entry on the documentation page include the following information:

FIRST SENTENCE

The first "sentence" contains the relied upon author's last name and the initials of his or her first and middle names. It usually includes the year the subject work was published enclosed in in parenthesis. A period ends this first "sentence."

SECOND SENTENCE

The second "sentence" includes the full title of the relied upon work, including any subtitles, appropriately printed in italic font (or set out in quotation marks or underlining if computer formatting is not available, which is highly unlikely). Some styles require specialized capitalization of certain titles to distinguish between book and article titles, and journal titles. Also, any editor's or translator's name would be here. A period ends this second "sentence."

THIRD SENTENCE

The third "sentence" offers all the pertinent publishing information, including the city and state, or country of publication and the publisher's name. Paper and electronic publications are treated differently, and the use of a reliable web-address or DOI (digital object identifier) number may also be placed here. Usually (although not always) this final "sentence" ends with a period.

The differences between the four major manuscript styles and the myriad of intricate variations within the styles themselves, have driven generations of students to utter distraction. You will be in some very good company if you find yourself overcome with frustration as you attempt to negotiate the twists and turns of academic documentation. However, you are or will soon be a college educated person; you are trained for trouble. Mastering documentation details is possible, and you possess the skills to be the master of them. Difficult, seemingly incomprehensible problems are precisely what educated persons are expected to solve, and like it or not, you are among that number of persons. If need be, get angry, set your intellectual teeth on edge, and do not loosen your jaw until you have triumphantly reduced every research paper complexity to simplicity.

***

Chapter Twelve Nutshell

Formal research writing is the beloved child of absent-minded professors everywhere. Students, on the other hand, will rarely use the words "beloved" and "research writing" in the same sentence. The four major research writing formats listed here are intensely complex paradigms. Of all the chapters in this volume, Chapter Twelve must announce that it is a surface-scratching chapter only. College level research writing demands specialized study from a format-dedicated text. Student research paper writers, be advised.

Chapter Twelve Exercise

The collateral reading in each of the previous chapter exercises is being relaxed here, partly because the student should be given some small degree of theme choice, and partly because the author's store of short, idea-crammed examples is temporarily exhausted. Accordingly, the student should select an appropriately idea-constituted theme and compose an essay response not exceeding 100 words which gives the theme its due. In the absence of a ready theme, reliance upon a published work of special interest to the student is recommended. Do not use direct quotation or paraphrase from any source.

AFTERWORD

I am not sure I can declare this volume a success. Its success would depend upon whether and to what extent your writing has improved and I have no way of knowing that first hand. To date, there is no indication of skyrocketing sales, and my publisher has not asked me to dinner, so it is safe to assume that it is and may remain a "quiet" book. Nevertheless, if you have found something in it that sticks to your compositional ribs, I am content.

As promised in the Foreword, the final note belongs to my bride. Throughout the two years it has taken to complete this volume she has relentlessly continued in her quest to make her husband a better man. I do not know for sure that she has succeeded in this, and I am reasonably certain that in several areas she has failed miserably, but she has tried her darnedest. If you apply yourself to your writing with half so good a heart as she has dedicated herself to my redemption, you are doomed to succeed.

Danbury, Connecticut
July 24, 2017
WILLIAM P. DE FEO

AUTHOR'S GLOSSARY

aberration	– unexpected negative result
affect	– to influence or impact
akin	– likened to
albeit	– however
amorphous	– without shape or definition
ampersand	– a symbol representing "and"
anathema	– in bitter opposition to
ancestral	– of one's deceased relations
anthropomorphic	– human traits to animals
appellations	– the names of
arcane	– unusual or old fashioned
assurance	– personal guarantee
astray	– away from the proposed path
astute	– of a superior mind
atomistic	– reduced to smallest particles
attenuated	– stretched out past recognition
axiom	– an unimpeachable truth
blatant	– in a rude or loud manner
capital	– money invested for gain

chapels	– diminutive churches
cognoscenti	– people of great learning
comedic	– relating to comedy
commendation	– notice of achievement
commodities	– useful products
complacency	– an air of indifference
comport	– to comply with or conform
concomitantly	– used at the same time as
condemn	– to proclaim guilty of wrong
conscientious	– a strong will to succeed
consequent	– as a result of
consonants	– letters other than vowels
consummate	– of absolute quality
conventional	– standard or ordinary
conversant	– person speaking with others
conversely	– opposite, in contradiction of
creed	– that believed in earnest
cryptic	– strangely mysterious
cunningly	– clever but suspicious manner
cursorily	– done without due preparation
decipher	– to render intelligible
decoding	– operation of reading
deconstruction	– deep, probing analysis
defused	– to relieve high stress
delineation	– a thorough review
demarcation	– a mark of location
demonstrably	– clearly obvious
diluted	– watered down to obscurity
discernable	– able to be seen, understood

discerning	– carefully thought out
disingenuous	– insincere, secretive
dispersed	– scattered into lesser parts
divers	– many in number
divine	– to determine the source of
dogged	– very determined
dross	– worthless residue
dynamics	– physical elements
embellish	– to exaggerate a description
endeavor	– to attempt or try to achieve
ephemeral	– short lived, not durable
epigram	– a short, witty saying
esoteric	– deeply dense and complex
exasperated	– maddening distress
excerpt	– a reduced portion
excruciating	– extreme pain, suffering
exemplary	– of the highest quality
explication	– complete explanation of
exponentially	– successive multiplication of
exposition	– explanation, instruction
extemporaneous	– provided without fore thought
faint	– of little or no strength
flabbergasting	– distressing confusion
forbearers	– deceased family members
fraught	– occurring or attended with
frivolous	– exceedingly unimportant
genus	– of a kind, type, or class
germane	– directly on point
gilded	– mere appearance of value

grudgingly	– done against one's will
harping	– annoying repetitive reference
idiosyncratic	– filled with minor flaws
immutable	– forever unchangeable
incumbent	– duty of or obligation to
inference	– a subtle suggestion of fact
interdependency	– relying each upon the other
intuit	– to know in advance of thought
irony	– utterly unanticipated result
jogging	– to loosen by shaking
litany	– a long annoying list of items
mammoth	– of huge proportion
melodic	– of or about a melody
myriad	– a large sample of
obfuscation	– words purposely misleading
pale	– to appear inferior to
palpable	– considerably evident, noticed
pedagogical	– of or relating to teaching
pedantic	– conceited teaching
peripatetic	– constantly moving
pesky	– irritating or annoying
phrasing	– musical interpretation
pith	– the essential element of
plethora	– a large number of
pretentious	– an arrogant, haughty attitude
problematic	– causing or given to trouble
prodigious	– large or significant
proficiency	– highest level of skill
proficiency	– possessing skill in

proximity	– in close relation to
purports	– claims to be capable of
quantum	– advanced physics
repudiation	– outright denial
resolute	– with clear purpose in mind
resonates	– perfectly aligned with
reverie	– a waking dream or fantasy
revision	– improve by modification
sauntering	– moving leisurely, slowly
scarcity	– in very short supply
shrink	– to nervously move away from
shrouded	– hidden from or veiled
sparingly	– used sparingly or seldom
sprawling	– large and spread out
staid	– quietly steady or sedate
staples	– chief elements, basic needs
static	– with motion, without change
strenuous	– requiring great strength
stylus	– hand-held writing devise
superfluous	– utterly unnecessary
tactile	– known by touch
tangible	– known through the senses
tedium	– extreme boredom
temerity	– rash, arrogant, bold
treatise	– a formal learned writing
twain	– both of, or two
unambiguous	– unable to be misunderstood
unrelenting	– not coming to an end
untutored	– not known of or about

valentine	– object of affection
venerable	– respected and honored
verbatim	– word for word record
vile	– evil, cruel, or vicious
whet	– to tempt or lead on to
willy-nilly	– with little or no interest
winnow	– to separate out, divide

WORKS CITED

Brooks, Gwendolyn. "Piano After War" in *Selected Poems.* Perennial Classics, 1999.

de Maupausant, Guy. "The Necklace" in *The Complete Short Stories of Guy de Maupassant.* P. F. Collier and Son, 1903.

Dickens, Charles. *A Tale of Two Cities.* Barnes and Noble Inc, 2004.

Donne, John. "Holy Sonnet No. 10" in *Collected Poems of John Donne.* Wordsworth Editions LTD, 1994.

Holmes, J. Oliver, W. McBoyle v. United States. (283 US 25).

Madison, James. "Federalist No. 10" in *The Federalist Papers.* Signet Classics Inc., 2003.

Montainge, Michel. *Selected Essays by Montaigne* (trans. by Wm. Hazlitt). Random House Inc., 1949.

Plato. "Crito" in *The Dialogues of Plato* in *Plato Complete Works.* Hackett Publishing Inc. 1997.

Shakespeare, William. "Hamlet" in *Complete Works of William Shakespeare*. Barnes and Noble, Inc., 2010.

Shakespeare, William. "The Merchant of Venice" in *Complete Works of William Shakespeare*. Barnes and Noble, Inc., 2010.

Swift, Jonathan. "Meditation upon a Broomstick" in *A Modest Proposal and Other Satirical Works*. Dover Publications Inc., 1996.

Whitman, Walt. "When I Heard the Learn'd Astronomer" in *Walt Whitman – The Complete Poems*. Penguin Publishing Group, 2005.

INDEX

NOTES

NOTES

NOTES

NOTES

NOTES

NOTES

NOTES

NOTES